THE

FIELD&
STREAM

RIFLE MAINTENANCE
H A N D B O O K

THE
FIELD & STREAM
RIFLE
MAINTENANCE
HANDBOOK

TIPS, QUICK FIXES, AND GOOD HABITS FOR EASY GUNNING

CHRIS CHRISTIAN

The Lyons Press
Guilford, Connecticut
An imprint of The Globe Pequot Press

To buy books in quantity for corporate use
or incentives, call **(800) 962–0973**
or e-mail **premiums@GlobePequot.com**.

The Lyons Press is an imprint of The Globe Pequot Press.

10 9 8 7 6 5 4 3 2 1

Printed in the United States of America

Designed by Mimi LaPoint

ISBN 978-1-59921-000-1

Library of Congress Cataloging-in-Publication Data is available on file.

GEARING UP 1

With the proper tools,
maintaining a rifle isn't difficult.

Any job is easier with the right tools. When it comes to maintaining a rifle, this is doubly important because trying to make do with marginal tools, lubricants and cleaning chemicals, or using them incorrectly, can damage the rifle. At the very least, they can severely degrade its accuracy or reliability.

After 35 years of visiting, working in, and just generally hanging around gun shops, I've come to the unfortunate conclusion that too many gun owners spend too much money and fuel in their quest to assemble effective equipment and materials. I'm sure that statement may irk many a gun shop owner, but it's not meant to be an insult—just an observation of current marketing realities.

Cleaning equipment is necessary, but it's hardly glamorous or exciting. Moreover, it takes up both valuable display space and inventory dollars to put on showroom shelves. The result is that most shops will have some basic solvents and oils and a modest selection of blister-packed "universal" cleaning kits. Many are not going to devote the cash flow and display space to the type of equipment that you routinely find in the gun rooms of knowledgeable shooters.

Unless the gun shop owner is a real aficionado himself and has a strong enough market base to support the inventory, you are not likely to find anything other than mass-merchandise items. I have had even poorer luck at the so-called Big Box stores, both in merchandise available and the knowledge of the store personnel. Other than the price of the item, their information has always been of limited value, and that is reflected in the mass-merchandise items they stock.

You don't need a lot of equipment to maintain a rifle properly. But you do need the proper gear, and of good quality. The easiest way to acquire it is to obtain a current copy of the Brownells catalog. If you are friendly with a competent gunsmith, you might be able to use his, as most are likely to have one. Their excellent selection, and availability of Internet or telephone orders, make them a useful and attractive source.

Brownells offers a wide selection of upper level cleaning equipment that is not always carried by your local gun shop.

Regardless of whether you use Brownells or another source for your supplies, here's a look at what you will want to have on your cleaning bench to keep your rifle operating at its peak.

CLEANING TOOLS

There are plenty of inexpensive, three-piece, screw-together cleaning rods on store shelves, but this is not what you want to use for normal cleaning. Not only can they flex and rub inside the bore, but regardless of the material from which they are made (usually aluminum or brass), they tend to break at the threaded junctions when pressure is applied, and some cleaning situations require pressure.

Instead, opt for a quality one-piece rod with a freely rotating handle. The better models will accept an adaptor at the business end that allows the use of a wide variety of tips. These are available in stainless steel, polymer, or nylon-coated; I prefer the coated models. There are a number of quality one-piece rods on the market which don't flex, don't break, and apply pressure properly. I have a rod made by J. Dewey Manufacturing that is almost 20 years old and in perfect condition. I paid more for it than a cheap three-piece set cost at the time, but I would have undoubtedly gone through several of the latter during the intervening time period. Don't skimp on the cleaning rod, because a $20 to $40 rod is not nearly as expensive as a new $300 barrel.

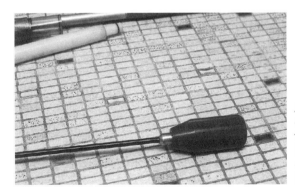

A quality one-piece cleaning rod with a freely rotating handle is the professional's choice for effective barrel cleaning.

Speaking of expensive barrels, once you have a quality cleaning rod invest a few more bucks and get a bore guide. This is an inexpensive component that fits into the chamber (on bolt action rifles that are best cleaned from the breech end), or over the muzzle (on pumps, lever actions, and those semi-autos that must be cleaned from the muzzle). You don't really need one for break-open single-shot firearms. Its purpose is to allow the rod to enter the bore smoothly, and keep it centered. On a bolt action gun it replaces the bolt. This not only lets the rod slide into the bore with minimal opportunity to nick the throat area, but also keeps solvent, crud, and dirty patches out of the all-important trigger assembly.

It is even more important to use a bore guide on rifles that must be cleaned from the muzzle. The muzzle crown is critical for accuracy and is precisely cut to allow the bullet to exit the barrel with equal gas pressure on all sides of its base. If the crown becomes nicked or damaged, that nick can allow propellant gas to squirt through it and create unequal gas pressure

The muzzle crown can be nicked or damaged, and that will adversely affect accuracy. A bore guide is strongly recommended if your barrel needs to be cleaned from the muzzle end.

A bore guide (or muzzle guide if your barrel needs to be cleaned from the front end) is inexpensive insurance against barrel damage.

that can actually tip the bullet slightly upon exit. This results in reduced accuracy, and ham-fisted cleaning from the muzzle end can be the cause of crown damage. A muzzle guide prevents this.

A gunsmith can re-cut a damaged crown, but a muzzle guide is cheaper. If you ever attend a major high-power rifle match, you will see virtually every competitor who is cleaning his or her rifle from the muzzle using one. They are that important for maximum accuracy.

You'll also need tips for the rod, and while there is a large selection on the market, you won't need very many. When it comes to brushes, most cleaning chores can be handled with a plain bronze bristle brush. Bronze is soft enough not to mar the bore, but sturdy enough to remove loosened powder fouling—which is all it needs to do most of the time. Make certain that the brush is properly sized to the bore. Trying to scrub a .30 caliber bore with a .22 caliber brush is not only a waste of time, but the undersized brush can allow the rod to contact the bore and some degree of damage could result. Bronze brushes are inexpensive, so you may as well buy several in each caliber you need. They don't last forever, and a worn brush is an undersized one.

There are also a number of different styles of stainless-steel bristle brushes on the market, and I generally avoid them. They are hard enough to scratch a bore, and even a microscopic scratch can become a magnet for jacket fouling. The only exception is if

A bronze brush (center) is the best bet for most barrels, while the spiral steel brush (upper) is very useful for lead-bullet shooters. The steel bristle brush (lower) is more useful for handguns than rifle bores.

lead bullets are used; in this case, a spiral-wound steel brush (some makers call it a tornado brush) is valuable. Lead sometimes has to be mechanically removed, and a bronze brush lacks the power to do much more than scrape a little bit off the top at a time. The spiral steel brushes will grab and move a lot more lead, and their spiral-wound design minimizes the chance of scratching the bore.

Most cleaning kits include a tip with a slot in it to hold a patch. When it comes to cleaning a barrel, these have little value. Some shooters believe that you can put in a patch, soak it with solvent, and then run it back and forth through the bore to remove crud. It doesn't work like that.

The patch itself isn't going to remove fouling until the chemicals and brush have a chance to loosen it, and the fit of the patch in the bore with a slot tip is usually too loose to push much anyway. All you accomplish when you do this is to move crud around inside the bore without removing it. About the only use for a slot tip in rifle cleaning is to saturate the bore with a solvent. When it comes time to actually remove the debris, you want a jag tip.

Jags are blunt-nosed tips that push a patch through the bore. If the patch is cut to the proper size, you get maximum patch-to-bore contact, with enough mechanical power to push crud out. A brush will loosen debris, and a jag with a tight-fitting patch removes it. If I had to clean with only one tip, it would be a jag. It's the most useful tip you can have.

You can find these in a number of different styles and made from several different materials. I favor a compact, blunt tip made from Nylon or aluminum. Both materials are tough enough for the job, and neither will scratch the bore, but the real reason for using these materials relates to solvents. If you are using a copper solvent (which will be explained in a moment) and use a jag made of brass or bronze, the solvent can pick up copper traces from those jags since both materials contain copper. This will give you a false reading on the cleanliness of your barrel.

Jags don't have to be perfectly sized to the bore. It's the fit of the patch that determines contact. If you are cleaning a .17 caliber you will definitely need one sized to that bore because the others are too big, but that jag will clean .22 caliber bores as well. A .22 caliber jag will effectively handle bores up to the .25 calibers. Add a jag sized for .270 caliber and another one for .35 caliber, and that small selection will let you handle all bores up to .45 caliber simply by cutting the patch to fit.

A bronze brush, blunt tip jag, and a slot tip will handle most barrel cleaning chores.

If you are one of the growing number of Cowboy Action shooters who routinely fire lead bullets, one last tip you'll want is a Lewis Lead Remover, available in an inexpensive kit from Brownells. This is a rubber bore-sized tip that fits a standard cleaning rod and holds a brass patch. If chemicals won't get the lead out, this will do it mechanically. Brass is softer than steel (so it won't scratch the bore), but harder than lead and will physically scrub it out. One potential problem with the Lewis Lead Remover is that the rubber plug supporting the replaceable brass patch may be a touch too big, preventing it from entering the bore. The solution is simply to sand it down a bit until you can get it in the bore. You only have to do it once, if at all, but once you get the tip properly fit to your bore, it is an excellent tool for removing stubborn leading that chemicals don't get out.

The above tools will take care of the bore. There is more that needs cleaning, however, and a proper parts brush is also nice to have. Hoppe's makes a good bronze-bristle one for a few bucks (there are others as well), and it can make quick work of removing crud and grit from action parts, extractors, and other small areas. When it comes to cleaning extremely close-tolerance parts like a trigger assembly, a plain old toothbrush is best—you don't want to leave a shed bronze bristle in there.

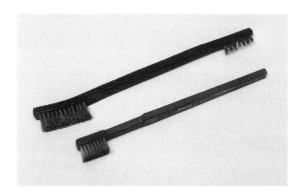

Parts brushes make short work of cleaning the interior action parts. The author favors a toothbrush (lower) for very close tolerance areas.

One last brush you shouldn't be without is a chamber brush. One might think that if the barrel has been scrubbed the chamber would also be clean, but that's not always the case. The chamber is a lot bigger than the bore, and seldom gets proper cleaning from bore brushes. A chamber brush is a short bristle brush on a flexible handle that allows you to scrub firing residue from the chamber area. If you shoot a pump, semi-auto, or lever action, a clean and dry chamber is important for proper feeding and extraction. A chamber brush is the best way to assure that, and it is not expensive.

You will also need cloth cleaning patches, and these are readily available just about anywhere gun-related items are sold. They can be had in bulk packs, or in blister packs "pre-cut" for certain caliber ranges. I normally avoid the latter because trying to keep the proper size on hand for various calibers is a pain in the logistics, and they often don't provide a tight fit. The bulk pack allows me to take a pair of scissors and cut patches to the exact size I want for whatever the intended chore is. You also don't need to purchase any of the "super wonderful high-tech durable" patches. A cloth patch is a single-use item. After it's been through the bore once, it goes in the garbage can. That patch is going to be dirty and there is no point in putting a dirty patch into a bore you want cleaned.

Cotton swabs are also handy. When combined with rubbing alcohol they are a very effective way to clean oil and crud out of screw holes and other hard-to-reach areas.

A few cotton swabs and some rubbing alcohol are the best way to clean oil and sludge from screw holes so that the thread locker can take a solid bite.

CLEANING SOLVENTS

There are two basic types of bore-cleaning compounds: chemicals and abrasives. Both are perfectly safe to use in any rifle barrel, and both will work. Depending on the type of projectile used, however, one type will be a significantly better choice for some cleaning chores than others.

Chemical cleaners are a blend of ingredients formulated to attack and dissolve, on a molecular level, specific types of fouling, which can then be removed with a jag/patch. They are my first choice when cleaning a barrel that fires jacketed bullets (and for some lead bullet cleaning) because they do a superb job, with little mess, and with minimal brush use that might score the barrel, throat or crown.

The most effective use of chemical solvents for cleaning a copper-jacket-fouled bore involves applying two different types. The first is a plain powder solvent. As their name implies, they attack powder fouling, although when left in a bore overnight they will often raise small bits of copper fouling. Two that I rely on are Hoppe's #9 and Outers Nitro Solvent. These are applied first to remove powder and primer fouling, because it's tough to get to the copper fouling until those are gone.

Once that is done, you can then apply dedicated ammonia-based copper solvent to remove the copper jacket fouling. Among those I have used with excellent results are Hoppe's Bench Rest, Gunslick Copper Klenz, and Shooter's Choice Copper Remover.

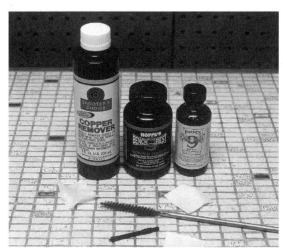

Bores firing jacketed bullets are best cleaned with a two-solvent approach that uses both powder and copper solvents, and minimal brush work.

Shooter's Choice is the most powerful and aggressive of the three and it is important to read and follow the directions carefully. It will pull copper fouling when nothing else can.

There was a time when ammonia-based copper solvents were somewhat controversial. Some experts loved them and others hated them . . . in fact, I have spoken with a couple of custom rifle smiths, who specialize in accuracy tune-ups, who will not work on a rifle if it has had ammonia-based solvents in the bore.

Such solvents can cause barrel damage if they are incorrectly used, and during their early days the information on their proper use was not widely disseminated. When used correctly, however, they work wonders on copper fouling, and using them properly is easy once shooters understand the nature of ammonia.

It has been written that ammonia-based solvents form an acid in the bore that will attack the metal, but that's not totally correct. What actually happens is that ammonia and atmospheric moisture will combine to form ammonia hydroxide. That's not an acid; it's a mild alkaline. It can, however, still etch the bore. If there are microscopic pits or cracks present, the ammonia hydroxide can widen them and create rough spots and pits within the bore that will trap and build up fouling, and this can degrade accuracy.

But—and this is critical—ammonia hydroxide only forms if the solvent is allowed to dry in the bore and remain there long enough for atmospheric moisture to combine with it. As long as the solvent is wet, ammonia hydroxide does not form, no adverse reaction takes place, and the only thing attacked is the copper fouling.

That was not adequately explained to many shooters, and they treated it just like the powder solvents they had been using all their lives. Many let it sit in the bore overnight, and some even left it in the bore as a preservative which is commonly done with some popular powder solvents that do not contain ammonia.

That did cause some bore damage, but the obvious answer is not to let the solvent dry in the bore, and that is the reason why most maker's instructions state it shouldn't sit there for more than a few minutes.

That doesn't mean, however, that you have to rush your cleaning. The key is not to let the solvent dry in the bore, and one way to give it more time to work is to re-wash the bore with fresh solvent every five minutes or so. As long as the solvent is wet, you can leave it in the bore as long as you want.

Once the copper fouling is removed, the residual copper solvent has to go, and dry-patching the bore isn't effective in thoroughly removing it. You need to flush it out. Plain water (wet a patch), oil, or spray degreasers will take it out, as will any powder solvent. Some makers add a few additional ingredients to their ammonia solvents that they claim will buffer any harmful effects. Regardless of which ammonia solvent I'm using, I always finish up with several wet powder solvent patches to clean it out, dry-patch out the powder solvent, and then oil the bore. Once this is understood, copper solvents are perfectly safe to use and the best way to remove copper fouling.

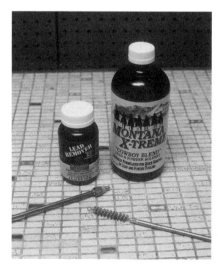

Lead-bullet shooters will find their cleaning tasks easier with dedicated lead solvents, a spiral steel brush, and a Lewis Lead Remover.

If you shoot lead bullets, the same two-solvent approach will also work if the leading isn't severe, but you dispense with the copper solvent and use one specifically formulated for lead. Shooter's Choice Lead Remover and Montana Xtreme "Cowboy Blend" are the best I have found.

In recent years there have been a number of new bore cleaners introduced that are referred to as "multi-purpose." They are billed as removing powder, copper, lead, and plastic fouling. Among them are Butch's Bore Shine, Shooter's Choice MC#7 and their Xtreme Clean, Hoppe's Elite, Birchwood Casey Bore Scrubber, Gunslick Ultra Klenz, and others. Some contain ammonia and some don't. All will work, and I go through these by the gallon on the handguns I use for action pistol competition. I don't often use them on rifles, however. In my experience they are not as effective for cleaning lead fouling, and definitely not moly, as are other methods. I am also not yet convinced that they will deep-clean a jacketed-bullet barrel as well as the two-chemical approach described above. They are a quicker way to clean, and I will sometimes use them if only a modest number of rounds have been fired, I'm pressed for time, and if I anticipate shooting that rifle again soon. But if I want to be certain I have that barrel scrubbed down to bare metal, the two-chemical approach is preferable.

Abrasive cleaners are the other option and they contain few chemicals. They contain an oil, wax, or grease base mixed with an extremely fine mix of abrasive ingredients like gypsum, chalk, clay and other inorganic substances. They clean by mechanically scouring fouling from the bore. Those I can recommend are J-B Bore Cleaning Compound, Iosso Bore Cleaner Paste, and Remington 40-X Bore Cleaner. To be truly effective, these need to be used in conjunction with a penetrating oil that will penetrate and lift much of the soft fouling before the paste is applied. The only oil I would use here is Kroil.

Shooters using moly-coated bullets will find the penetrating oil/bore paste abrasive method their best bet.

Abrasives will work on jacketed or slightly fouled lead bullet barrels, although not as well as the chemical system. If you are shooting moly-coated bullets, however, you will want to use abrasives. They do a much better and quicker job than chemicals when it comes to moly fouling.

OTHER SOLVENTS YOU'LL NEED

The bore is only one part of the rifle that needs to be routinely cleaned. Action parts, bolt faces, trigger groups, and the gas systems on gas-operated semi-autos also need care, and require different solvents for the easiest and most effective cleaning.

Gas-operated semi-autos often have carbon buildup on certain action parts, especially those components that are bombarded with propellant gases. This is tough to remove with bore

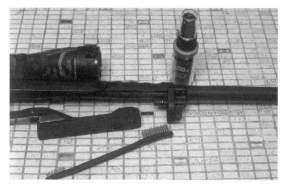

Gas port systems are often overlooked, but they can build up a lot of carbon that can impede functioning.

solvents. Break-Free Carbon Cutter is specifically formulated to handle this. I have also had pretty good results with Hoppe's Elite Gun Cleaner. If you shoot this type of rifle you'll want one of them on hand.

Small, hard-to-reach areas, especially if they involve close-tolerance parts like trigger assemblies, are most easily handled with a spray degreaser. Just about every company that makes gun solvents will offer one and I have had good success with Birchwood Casey Gun Scrubber and Shooter's Choice Polymer Safe Degreaser. These are pressurized aerosols that blow crud and oil out of tiny places, and they do a good job. Their drawback is cost, especially if you use a lot of it, as I do. For that reason I generally use carburetor spray. The house brand sold by the Advance Auto Parts chain (Advance Auto Parts Carb & Choke Cleaner) is the most effective I've found and I can buy four 16-ounce cans for what one of the "gun specific" sprays cost. I go through a can every two weeks, so it does add up.

Whichever spray is used, you don't want to use it in the house. The fumes are annoying and flammable. I take the parts I want to spray, put them in a plastic tray lined with paper towels, step out onto the back porch, and blast away. If they need brush work I do it out there. I don't mind my gun room smelling like Hoppe's No. 9 (in fact, I wish someone could capture that scent in an aftershave), but the degreasers are a bit much.

Once they are sprayed, I shake them to remove as much solvent as I can and then bring them back in and lay them out to air dry, which can take hours. The wait is necessary because if you apply lubricant to them while they are still wet with the degreaser it does little good—the degreaser eats it. And you do need to lube them because the degreaser strips the metal of any lubrication and protection from rust.

Another excellent but overlooked use for these sprays is in cleaning bore brushes and parts brushes. When you run a brush through a solvent-soaked bore it collects fouling. If you don't re-move it, you'll add some to the bore the next time you use that brush. The sprays not only keep them clean, but also extend their life. The same holds true for parts brushes. There's no rea-son to use a dirty brush to try and clean something.

LUBRICANTS AND PRESERVATIVES

Metal-on-metal moving parts require some type of lubrication, both for proper function and to prevent excessive wear. After a rifle has been properly cleaned it should be lubricated because the cleaning process will have stripped out what was there.

This is where a lot of gun owners become their own worst enemy. Some feel that if a little oil is good, a lot is better. In re-ality, the opposite is true, and excessive or incorrect lubrication is one of the primary causes of malfunctions. Lubricants do smooth metal-on-metal movement, but they can also capture and hold powder and primer fouling, along with dust, dirt, and other normal field debris. Add this to oils and grease, and it forms an abrasive paste, as well as a crud buildup, that can prevent moving parts from seating properly. If you combine this with cold weather, you also get a "sludge" that can literally bring the oper-ating action to a grinding halt. Some types of lubricants display this propensity more than others, and it is critical to use them on the proper parts of the rifle to avoid problems.

The basic and most common-sense rule of lubricants is: "The tighter the tolerances and the smaller the parts, the lighter the lube required. The bigger the parts and the looser the toler-ances, the heavier the lube required." Light lube translates to light oil, while heavy lube translates to grease. Both have uses on a rifle. But just because the can says "oil" doesn't mean it's the best choice in that area, and the same goes for "grease." The best light oils I have found are Corrosion X For Guns and Shooter's

Choice FP-10 Lubricant Elite. Both have a viscosity level not much heavier than water (which allows them to flow freely into tight places), and both will form a polar bond with the metal.

When it comes to applying the proper lubrication to trigger groups, firing pins, extractor springs, and virtually any other part of the internal action or safety levers, these are my first choices. A few drops applied to the part will flow freely into the surfaces, and once the action is dry-cycled a couple of times it's covered.

Although they are light oils, I have no problem using them for some heavier-duty applications as well. In fact, Corrosion X is what I lube the contact between frame and slide rail on my semi-auto action pistols, and when you can rapid fire thirty rounds in thirty seconds on a hot August day in Florida without a malfunction, you know the lube works. And at the other temperature extreme, it won't gum up when temperatures dip below freezing.

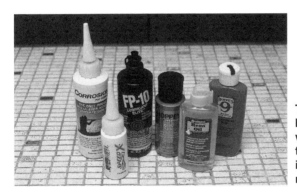

There are a number of light gun oils available which will provide all the lubrication that internal action parts require.

If you can't find these, then a light gun oil (like Remington Rem Oil, Outers Scent Out Lube Oil Lubricant, or Hoppe's Elite Gun Oil) will work on tight parts as long as they're used sparingly. One "oil" that should not be used in firearm lubrication is WD-40. It's popular with some but it's not a true lubricant—it's a penetrating oil designed to loosen stuck parts, not effectively lubricate them. Nor does it work as well as others as a rust preventative.

Greases also have a role, particularly in pumps, lever actions, semi-autos, and some single-shot rifles. But you want to use one formulated for the heat and pressure that firearms generate. A bucket of hardware store grease isn't. Those specifically designed for firearms that I have used with good results are Tetra Gun Grease, Shooter's Choice All Weather High-Tech Grease, and Sentry Hi-Slip Grease.

Preventing rust on a firearm, be it external or interior to the barrel, can be a chore for those in humid climates, and a good rust preventative is a major asset. Both Corrosion X and FP-10 are excellent in that regard when applied to a cloth and spread over external surfaces or swabbed through a bore, but there are several more easily used aerosol sprays available. Among those that have a solid track record are Brownells Rust Preventative No. 2, Birchwood Casey Barricade, Tetra Gun L, and Shooter's Choice Rust Prevent.

Periodic maintenance should include removing the action from the stock and coating the hidden metal areas with a quality rust preventative.

One last chemical compound you'll want on hand is a liquid thread locker. Every gun has screws; some more than others. Recoil and vibration can loosen any of them, and nothing good happens when that occurs. A small tube of Loctite Medium Strength Thread Locker (blue formula) can prevent a lot of that. There are other, similar products available and they also work well. The medium-strength formula is best for gun work, as it holds well and the bond can be broken with hand tools. The permanent formulas (usually a red liquid) should not be used because you may not be able to easily get that screw out at a later date.

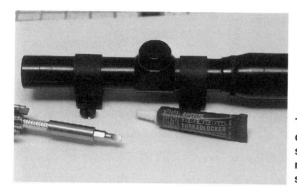

Thread locker and a quality hollow ground screwdriver are a must for keeping screws tight.

BENCH TOOLS

Ask any gunsmith what his biggest repair pet peeve is, and he will probably tell you it's damaged screw heads from shooters using improper screw drivers. (The rest will likely be split between shooters using a permanent thread locker, and those engaging in over-lubrication).

Hollow-ground bits are the screwdrivers used for gun work. Straight-tapered tips are the ones you find for general use in the hardware store. The advantage to hollow-ground bits is that they transmit all of the energy created from the twisting motion up the shank of the bit and to the screw head. They also provide a much better metal-to-metal fit between the driver bit and screw, which goes a long way in preventing burrs in the screw heads. The tapered design transmits the energy to the edge of the screw slot and actually tends to force the bit out of the slot. You can tell if a tapered bit has been used a lot on a gun screw because you will see where it has actually rolled up metal on each end of the screw slot. A properly fit hollow-ground bit won't do that.

If you're going to be adjusting any of the screws on your gun, I strongly recommend that you have the proper screwdrivers to do it with. In addition to the considerations already described, hollow-ground screwdrivers intended for the gunsmith trade are invariably made of higher-grade steel than the inexpensive hardware store tapered models. This minimizes the chance of a bit breaking on a stubborn screw and gouging your gun. Gunsmith-grade, hollow-ground screwdrivers are available from Brownells, and individual drivers to fit specific screws can be purchased. Some auto parts stores and large department stores will also have hollow ground drivers, often in the form of a multi-tool with interchangeable bits. These are convenient and will generally work well. I have one that gets a lot of use.

Drift punches are another important but often-forgotten item. Many guns use through pins to hold parts assemblies, particularly some pump and semi-autos that rely on them to retain trigger groups. A thorough cleaning often requires that these parts be removed, and a drift punch does it much more effectively than banging on a screwdriver. One or two drift punch sizes should handle most chores, and they are not expensive.

Lastly, you'll need some type of fixture to properly hold and support the rifle while you scrub the bore and perform other routine maintenance chores. Trying to juggle a rifle in one hand while you manipulate a cleaning rod with the other is not only awkward, but creates the potential for damage. It's difficult to keep a bore or muzzle guide in place in this manner; it can cause even a quality rod to flex and contact the bore. And there is also the very real possibility of losing your grip on the rifle and dropping it—which can damage the scope or sights.

You're much better off if you have the rifle secured in a solid fixture that leaves both hands free, and—preferably—has the barrel pointing slightly downhill so that the muzzle is below the action. Regardless of whether you are cleaning from the muzzle or the breech, if the muzzle is higher than the action you will get solvents and debris flowing down the barrel and into the action. Keeping the muzzle at a lower elevations allows the excess solvent and crud you want out of your barrel to flow to the muzzle, which makes cleaning the action parts much easier.

There are a number of gun cradles on the market that will hold a rifle in the proper position. They are not only the best choice for cleaning a rifle, but also for adjusting scope mounts and other maintenance-related chores. Any gunsmith that does even minimal rifle work will have one. One model that impresses me is the Gunslick Match-Grade Gun Maintenance Center. This is made from injection molded plastic (very easy to clean), holds the gun securely fore and aft, and provides pull-out trays to hold brushes, tips and patches. It also includes molded indentations on the base that help keep chemical bottles from spilling. It's functional, inexpensive, and transports easily to the range if you require cleaning services there.

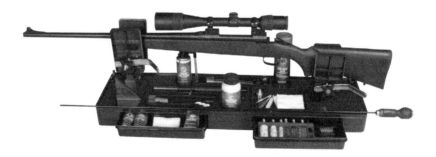

The Gunslick Match-Grade Gun Maintenance Center is an excellent answer to your rifle-cradling needs. It is equally well-suited for cleaning or maintenance tasks.

The drawback to the task-specific gun cradles is that's all they do—cradle the gun. They have no other real function, and most are not a suitable rest for sighting a rifle in. They also take up a fair amount of space in the gun room to perform that one function. If you have the room and want the best, by all means a gun cradle is the way to go.

A more versatile option is the Hughes Range Rest or their Bench Buddy. These are designed to serve as gun cradles to clean and work on the gun, while also functioning as solid rests to sight in a rifle. They're not expensive ($30 – $40) and do a good job at both tasks. They are, unfortunately, still fairly large pieces

Two products from Hughes—their Range Rest (top) and Bench Buddy (left)— are inexpensive and versatile solutions for your cleaning, maintenance and sight-in needs.

of equipment and I don't have the room to dedicate to them. My cleaning bench is far too cluttered, and I am shifting constantly among rifles, shotguns and handguns. I'm probably not alone in that regard, but there is a simple solution. I have a couple of short Harris bipods (the Benchrest Model BR and Prone Model

H), and attaching one to the front sling swivel lug makes a fine forward support. Slipping the buttstock onto my Hughes Ballistic Shooting Bag, or even a sturdy cardboard box with a V-shaped notch cut into it, provides effective rear support. The bag and bipod form a solid cleaning platform to properly support the rifle, and when done they store easily until it's time for them to go back to their normal duties as field equipment. I've always been a big fan of multiple-use equipment, so this system works well for me, and should also work for any other shooter.

A proper cleaning station supports the gun, with the muzzle pointing down, and leaves both hands free to work. A bipod and a rear bag is the author's choice, but there are others.

One rifle can be a significant investment. Several rifles can take a bunch of bucks. The most effective equipment and chemicals required to keep them clean, pristine, and in peak operating condition costs little more than "bargain basement" products. It makes sense to gear up right, and there's no good reason not to.

LOVE YOUR BARREL 2

If your barrel won't perform,
your rifle is virtually useless.

Every component on a rifle plays an important role in its overall level of performance. After all, no rifle is better than its trigger, and none will hit what the sights can't see. In the same vein, if the feeding mechanism is malfunctioning you have, at best, a single shot, while a poorly shaped stock may pound the shooter so badly that making an accurate shot becomes almost impossible.

Every component counts, but when you distill them down to their essence, their only real function is to allow the barrel to precisely direct a bullet to the target. If the barrel isn't capable of that, the rest of the rifle becomes moot. Experienced shooters who demand peak accuracy regard a good barrel as the most important component on the rifle. It's also the easiest to maintain in peak condition. Unfortunately, it's also the easiest to neglect. And, if that neglect is severe enough, even a top-quality barrel can quickly go bad.

Veteran shooters consider barrel care to be one of the most important maintenance chores they can perform, and that proper care starts before they ever put the first round down the bore.

BREAKING IN A NEW BARREL

The first thing shooters want to do with a new rifle is shoot it. That's just human nature—bring that shiny new firearm to the range, pound a couple of boxes of ammo through it, and see what it'll do.

If, however, you ever want to realize the maximum accuracy potential of the rifle, and enjoy a long barrel life, that's the worst thing you can do to it. Any rifle barrel needs a certain degree of breaking in before it is capable of delivering peak performance, and the reason for that is fairly simple.

There are essentially two types of rifle barrels available today: factory barrels and custom match barrels. Factory barrels are mass-produced, installed on the action, test fired, and the rifle is then shipped. If you look down the bore of a factory barrel with a quality bore scope you will see machine marks (most running across the lands) and other rough areas inside the bore. If these are not properly smoothed out they act like a rasp every time a bullet goes down the barrel, and you will be pounding copper fouling (or lead, if that's your bullet of choice) into those blemishes. That results in inconsistent bore dimensions, and not only will accuracy ultimately suffer, but it will continue to deteriorate as fouling builds.

Match barrels normally receive some degree of barrel lapping prior to shipment, so machine marks and rough spots in the bore are minimal. The throat is another matter.

When the barrel is chambered there are minute machine marks created in the throat running across the lands, and they also act like a rasp. When the bullet is forced into the barrel, those machine marks generate a copper dust that mixes with the propellant gases and is carried down the bore. This is deposited into the bore, and since copper adheres very well to itself, a buildup occurs. It's not necessarily the result of a rough bore, but until the throat marks are smoothed out you'll get a copper fouling buildup. The same machine marks are also present in the throats of factory barrels, and the same thing occurs.

The purpose of breaking in a barrel is to allow the fired bullets to lap the bore and throat smooth, while not allowing any fouling to accumulate during that process. Some shooters wonder if that is really necessary. After all, the gun was shooting great right out of the box, so why does it need improvement? That logic may seem sound, but will the barrel continue to perform?

To observe a brand new barrel shooting well is not uncommon at all, and this can be true of both factory and custom match varieties. That's because there is minimal fouling that has thus far accumulated into the tool marks and rough spots within the bore. It hasn't built enough, so far, to degrade accuracy. But pounding round after round down a new bore does nothing more than weld copper or lead into those rough spots, where it will destroy accuracy and make it extremely difficult to ever get that barrel truly clean. It is not at all uncommon for a new barrel to shoot well at first, and then lose that accuracy in the future. If you break the barrel in properly, it will not only deliver the accuracy it is capable of now, but well down the road. Subsequent cleaning will also be much easier, and its accurate life will be extended.

The bottom line is that your new rifle may shoot minute-of-angle now, but it may lose that level of accuracy very quickly if it is not broken in. Breaking in a new rifle barrel is a tedious and time-consuming chore, and the good news is that it starts before you ever fire the first round.

Step one is to clean the "new" barrel down to bare metal before the first round goes down the bore. This is especially important with factory barrels because they will arrive with copper and powder fouling from the test firing, along with microscopic metal particles from the rifling process. If these aren't removed, subsequent firings do nothing more than grind them into the bore.

Since jacketed bullets are invariably the test rounds of choice, I favor chemical cleaning here. The first step is to thoroughly coat (wash) the bore with patches soaked in a quality powder solvent. You have to get the powder fouling out before you can truly attack the copper. I normally use Hoppes #9, and this is one of the few situations where I have any use for a slot tip on the cleaning rod. It's good for washing a bore, although not much else.

Get the bore thoroughly wet, and let it sit for a few minutes. Then shift to a proper-sized bronze bristle brush and work it vigorously back and forth through the bore ten or fifteen times. This helps loosen the powder fouling the solvent raised, and is also the last time I normally use a brush in this process. Every other step is chemical.

Once the bore has been brushed, shift to a jag tip with a tight-fitting, solvent-soaked patch and run it through the bore. This is a one-way trip—in one end and out the other. It makes no sense to run the patch back and forth through the bore because all you are doing is redistributing the crud. Repeat this step a few times and then run dry patches through; again on a one-way trip. If they come out white, the powder fouling is gone. If they're gray, wash the bore again and let it soak a few minutes before re-brushing and then push a few more wet patches through before shifting to dry patches. When the dry patches come out white (or with just a tinge of light gray), it's time for the copper solvent.

Wash the bore thoroughly with any one of the popular ammonia-based copper solvents and let that sit a few minutes before shifting to a jag tip with a copper-solvent-soaked patch, and making another one-way trip through the bore. Save the patch for examination.

When using copper solvents, do not use a bronze or brass jag tip. The only way (other than a quality bore scope) that you can tell if there is copper fouling in the bore is by examining the patch for the presence of bluish or greenish stains. This is the copper fouling lifted by the solvent. Brass and bronze contain copper, and the patch will often pick some up from the jag. This can give you a false reading. Many bench rest shooters use either plastic or aluminum jags because of this. That way, they know that if there is any copper wash on the patch it will be from the bore, and not a false reading from the jag tip.

Shooters using copper solvent need to use a plastic jag (upper) instead of the bronze jag (lower). The latter will transmit copper wash to the patch and provide false readings.

Repeat the bore wash and one-way patch procedure until the patches come out without any telltale blue or green stains. Then run a couple of powder-solvent patches through the bore to remove the copper solvent, and a couple of dry patches to finish up. Your barrel is now at bare metal, and you're ready to start shooting—but don't put away the cleaning gear yet. You'll be using it a lot.

Once the barrel is stripped clean, give the bore (but not the chamber) a light coat of gun oil, and fire one round of jacketed ammo. Some experts dispense with the oil, but others feel it is important not to run a dry bullet down a new dry bore. I agree with that, believing that a little lubrication helps reduce copper deposits.

After the first round is fired, repeat the entire "down to bare metal" cleaning procedure, re-oil the bore, and fire one more round. Then repeat the whole process again. Then, do it again, completing at least four of these cleaning cycles.

The one-round-then-clean procedure is a pain, but a necessary one at first. It provides maximum smoothing without allowing a copper fouling buildup. Just how many times this procedure should be done depends largely on what your copper solvent patches are telling you during cleaning. If you are getting a significant blue/green wash on the patch after firing only one round, this tells you the bore is still rough and is grabbing a lot of copper. Continue the one-round procedure until it abates. Most experts feel a minimum of ten rounds will be needed. Stainless-steel barrels generally break in more quickly than chrome-moly barrels, which seem to have a greater affinity for copper. Some chrome-moly factory barrels may need as many as twenty one-round cycles.

After the one-round cycles, don't put the ammo and cleaning gear away just yet. Shift to two or three round strings (cleaning between each string) until you have 35 – 40 total rounds through that barrel. After that, clean the barrel after every 12 – 15 rounds until you have about 150 total through it.

The above procedures will properly break in any centerfire rifle barrel, regardless of whether it will ultimately be firing copper-jacketed, moly-coated, or lead bullets. It is, admittedly, a tedious process. This is especially true on most public ranges. In fact, given the required cleaning time, it may be impossible to complete the task in one day at such a facility. Fortunately, it doesn't have to be done in one day. As long as each successive round is fired and the barrel then cleaned/oiled as described, it can be done over a period of weeks. Nor does it require a real range. You're not trying to score a target or sight in the gun; you're just putting rounds down the barrel between cleanings.

Any area with a safe back stop just a few yards down range, and a place to clean the gun, will do. There is also no point in using premium-grade ammo. The cheapest jacketed loads you can find are just fine.

An alternative method available to those that reload their own ammo is pressure lapping (sometimes called fire lapping). This involves handloading bullets that have been impregnated with abrasives, and firing them through the bore. By using progressively finer abrasive grits on the bullets, the barrel can be "lapped" to a state that equals, or exceeds, that of a custom match barrel. A number of professional rifle competitors and shooting teams use this method and are convinced it does a better job than using non-embedded bullets.

Two of the most effective kits to accomplish this are the NECO Pressure Lapping Kit, and David Tubb's Final Finish System. Both products are available in kit form with all required instructions, and are carried by Brownells. Either system takes time, and some shooters will be tempted to short-circuit the process. My philosophy is that since I'm only going to do it to that barrel once, I may as well do it right. The benefits are both immediate and long term.

By way of example, I got involved in predator control coyote hunting about fifteen years ago on a quasi-professional basis, and needed a rifle that would dunk a dog anywhere out to the 800-yard mark. Some of the central Florida cattle ranches that retained me had some huge pastures. That dictated an accurate gun, since bullet holes in cows and calves was considered a major no-no, not to mention leaving a large hole in my chronically underpowered wallet. I settled on a Winchester Model 70 Heavy Varminter in .243 Win and took the time to break it in. When I finished, the rounds it really liked would group around a quarter inch at 100 yards. The long-range handload I eventually developed would stay under an inch at 300 yards, and around 3.5

inches at 600 yards if the wind was down. Fifteen years, a few thousand rounds, and a pile of coyotes later, it'll still do that. The two days I took to break it in were well spent.

KEEP IT CLEAN

The fact that the gun shoots that well today reflects the break-in period. It also reflects proper routine cleaning on a regular basis. No matter how well you break in a barrel, copper jacketed fouling will still accumulate. If you let it lay there, it will eventually eat your barrel.

How often you need to clean is not carved in stone. When I was on a several-week trip I generally cleaned it every 30 – 40 rounds, because that was the point at which jacketed bullets began building up enough fouling to degrade accuracy. There were trips when the gun never reached that round count, and was not cleaned until I got back home. Some guns will function without adverse effects after longer round strings, and others need attention sooner. The only way to really know is to run some tests. Shoot successive groups over a period of several days (don't overheat the barrel in one session), and note your targets. The targets will tell you when the barrel needs a bath.

Once those coyote safaris were over, the gun was cleaned down to bare metal and the bore coated with CorrosionX. Copper, powder, and primer fouling, combined with normal atmospheric moisture (which we have in abundance in my home state of Florida) are not kind to barrels. Any hunter who doesn't thoroughly clean and oil the bore before the rifle is stored between seasons should not be surprised when he drags it out to sight in for the upcoming season, and finds it "doesn't shoot like it used to".

The chemical cleaning procedures outlined above (powder solvent first, light bronze brush use, then the copper solvent, with powder solvent to finish) will thoroughly scrub any properly maintained barrel using copper-jacketed bullets.

MOLY IS DIFFERENT

When I began shifting to moly-coated bullets, however, the cleaning procedures had to shift as well. Molybdenum disulfide is a

The most effective barrel-cleaning technique depends upon the bullet used in that bore. Jacketed bullets are best served with different chemicals than those that are effective on moly (center) or lead (right).

naturally occurring substance that is one of the slipperiest materials known to man. It has been used as a lubricant since the 1920s, but only recently has technology allowed it to be economically bonded to bullet jackets. Many custom bullet makers now offer their projectiles with moly coating, and there are some companies that will coat jacketed bullets shipped to them. Some of the major ammo makers also offer moly-coated bullets in their loaded ammunition lines.

Moly-coated bullets offer some advantages. One is that they greatly reduce the friction that occurs when a copper-clad bullet is driven down a steel barrel under high pressure and heat. The lesser friction does reduce bullet deformation and some shooters feel this produces more consistent accuracy levels. I'm not convinced of that—quality jacketed bullets can be just as accurate if the barrel is properly maintained. There is also evidence that moly bullets are less affected by wind, and show less wind drift than an identical bullet with just a copper jacket. My experience indicates there is some truth in that, but the difference isn't significant until you get out past the 500-yard mark, which few shooters do.

The biggest "no doubt about it" advantage, however, is that moly-coated bullets greatly reduce the copper fouling that degrades accuracy. Some will still occur, but not nearly what you'll get with a plain copper jacket. Savvy bench rest shooters will usually clean their bores every 10 – 20 rounds when using jacketed slugs in order to maintain peak accuracy, but many competitive shooters now find they can go as long as a couple hundred rounds with moly. My .243 needs cleaning every thirty-five or so rounds with jacketed slugs, or accuracy degrades. But I've hauled it out on a few western prairie dog hunts and run 250 – 300 rounds of moly bullets through it with no measurable loss of accuracy. Moly has become very popular with varmint hunters and competitive shooters for that reason. They shoot a lot of rounds, and the less time they have to spend cleaning the more time they get to spend shooting.

Moly also allows them to hang onto their barrel quite a bit longer. Depending upon the caliber, the maximum accuracy-life of a properly maintained centerfire rifle barrel shooting jacketed bullets may be as little as 1,000 rounds, and seldom more than 3,000. Those high-volume shooters who use moly exclusively have found that the reduced friction can more than double the accurate life of their barrels. That saves not only money, but also the time and aggravation required to break in and re-tune a new barrel.

That's the good news concerning moly-coated bullets. The bad news is that just running out and buying a box of them isn't going to do you any good. In fact, they probably won't equal the accuracy of the jacketed loads you're using now. Any rifle that's going to shoot moly-coated bullets has to have the barrel properly prepped for them. And, once prepped, you stay with moly.

Even a couple of jacketed bullets will "un-prep" it and put you back to square one.

Moly can't tolerate even minor amounts of copper fouling in the bore, and if there is any present the accuracy will suffer. Even with a fully scrubbed bore, maximum accuracy with moly won't occur until perhaps 10 – 20 rounds have been put through the gun to properly "season" the bore—much like a cast-iron skillet needs to be seasoned before use. You have to lay some moly fouling down in the bore.

Once the barrel is cleaned and seasoned, a couple of jacketed bullets will remove it all, and subsequent moly bullets are going to wander around until the rifle is scrubbed and seasoned again. This fact was not well understood by many shooters when moly bullets were first introduced, and it caused quite a few problems. More than a few hunters read about the "new" bullets and gave them a try without prepping the barrel. Accuracy was dreadful. Other hunters bought moly-coated ammo without even realizing it was different, and some of those loads quickly developed a poor reputation.

Had shooters understood the properties of moly, all that could have been avoided. And, once they were understood, many shooters would have realized they didn't even need moly. The casual deer hunter, who may not shoot forty rounds a year, isn't going to see any real benefit. In fact, he or she would be better off with jacketed slugs—cleaning is easier, and you can find plain jacketed loads anywhere ammo is sold.

Those that will realize the moly advantage are high-volume shooters who want to extend barrel life and be able to shoot more between cleanings. The latter is a good deal, because proper barrel cleaning with moly is not only different than with jacketed slugs, but also a bit messier.

The chemical method used for jacketed slugs doesn't work well with moly. This material lays down its own coating in the bore (the seasoning) that has to be removed before any copper fouling can be reached. The chemicals won't do it. Abrasives, combined with penetrating oil, are required—along with some elbow grease.

There are several recommended cleaning procedures for moly barrels, and all rely on abrasives and oil. The one that I have found to be the most effective is the one recommended by the folks at Berger Bullets, who have been at the forefront of the moly revolution since its beginning. It begins by pushing two successive Kroil-soaked patches on a jag through the bore, waiting a few minutes, and then following that with two successive dry patches. This will remove surface powder fouling, and start to soak through the moly to loosen it. Continue with two successive patches, soaked with Butch's Bore Shine, to wash the bore thoroughly. This is allowed to sit in the bore for five to ten minutes, to loosen and lift more crud.

Push two successive dry patches through, which will remove a lot of debris. After that, it's time for an abrasive bore paste like Iosso, J-B Bore Cleaning Compound, or Remington 40-X. The folks at Berger recommend the J-B Bore Cleaning Compound, but I have used the others with good results. This can be applied on a patch wrapped tightly around a long-toothed jag tip, or (as I do) on a long patch wrapped lengthwise along a bronze bristle

Abrasive pastes can be applied via a patch on a long jag or a bronze brush. The author prefers the brush because it provides a more consistent fit.

brush. I prefer the brush, because you have to wrap just the right amount of patch around the jag to get a tight bore fit: too little and you miss spots, too much and you can't get it into the bore. The brush, however, will compress, so even if the patch is oversized you'll still get it into the bore and achieve firm contact. It's simpler. You will also trash that brush with bits of patch material that you'll never get out, so dedicate that one brush to abrasive cleaning because it won't be good for anything else.

Coat the patch thoroughly and, using short back-and-forth strokes, work the paste through all portions of the bore to thoroughly scrub it. This isn't a one-way trip—you are physically scrubbing the barrel with the abrasive and it can take a bit of time to get a shiny, clean bore. You may also need to change patches if the first becomes too "gunked" or shredded. This is followed by several successive patches soaked with Kroil in order to remove the paste, and then cleaned up with three or four dry patches.

Fire five to ten of moly rounds to re-season the bore, and you're good to go for another couple hundred rounds. If the gun is going into end-of-season storage, however, I omit firing the rounds when I get down to shiny bore, and go to copper solvent. Patch this through until there is no copper washout, then clean the copper solvent out with powder solvent, oil the bore, and store. When the gun goes back into action you'll need ten to twelve moly rounds to season it.

When breaking in a new barrel that is to be used with moly bullets, you can do it either of two ways. The first is to use the same break-in and cleaning procedures you would for jacketed rounds, and use jacketed loads (they're cheaper); then clean it down to bare metal and run a dozen moly rounds down it to season. Or, you can clean the new barrel with the moly-abrasive method, fire one moly round, clean the barrel again, and repeat that five or six times. Then shift to three-round strings and clean between strings. Repeat that five or six times and finish with one last cleaning. Either method will work well.

GETTING THE LEAD OUT

Although not many use them anymore, there are still shooters who favor lead bullets (especially Cowboy Action competitors), and the most effective way to clean a leaded barrel involves yet a different cleaning procedure.

Before getting into that, let me state that I consider it critically important that a rifle barrel to be used with lead bullets be properly broken in—even more so than with the other two projectiles. Copper and moly are softer than steel, and will build up fouling in a rough bore. Lead is softer than either, and will build up fouling that much more. You can actually coat a bore with lead until it begins to resemble a smoothbore. With a properly broken-in barrel, there is less in the way of rough areas to strip lead, and that results in better accuracy and far easier cleaning. The break-in procedures listed above will work very well for lead if jacketed bullets are available for your caliber. Use them. If not, opt for the pressure lapping system (or lead bullets with copper gas checks). Lead, by itself, is not hard enough to lap a steel barrel, and trying to break one in with plain lead bullets accomplishes nothing other than to provide plenty of cleaning practice and eat up your ammo supply.

Once you get the barrel broken in, you can simplify the cleaning process if you use the proper lead bullet for the velocity levels you are achieving, and there are three basic types of lead bullets.

The first are swaged bullets. These are made by running a lead rod into a forming die. The resulting bullets are then coated with a dry outside lubricant. In order to form in the dies the lead has to be relatively soft, and swaged bullets are the softest lead projectiles commonly used. They will work quite well as long as velocities are kept below about 1,000 feet per second. Drive them faster than that and they can lead the barrel badly.

Swaged bullets have a limited role in rifles and I seldom use them there, although that's about all I feed the revolvers I use for action pistol competition. Their advantage is very low cost, while offering good performance at lower velocities. A number of Cowboy Action shooters using lever-action carbines in pistol calibers (.357, 44-40 and .45 LC) find them very satisfactory.

The next option is cast lead bullets. These are made by pouring molten lead into a mold, running the resulting bullet through a die to size it, and applying lubricant to external grooves on the bullet. The lead hardness can be increased by adding tin or antimony to the lead, and these are commonly called "hard cast" bullets. With the proper hardening agents, these can zip out at velocities up to about 1,600 feet per second before lead deposits get out of control.

The last option is a hard cast bullet with a copper gas check on the base. The addition of the gas check allows velocities to be cranked up to as much as 2,300 feet per second, and they actually produce the least amount of leading. The copper gas check tends to strip a lot of leading from the barrel upon firing, although—unlike plain lead bullets—it will leave some degree of copper fouling in the bore that must be removed.

Cleaning lead can be rather simple, or quite arduous. It depends upon the condition of the bore and whether or not the proper bullet is being used for the velocity of the load. In that respect, no two lead-bullet barrels are alike. Each will have its own quirks and may respond well to chemical cleaning, or require abrasives.

Chemical cleaning is the easiest, and is done almost like it would be for copper-jacketed bullets. The difference is that a solvent designed for lead is required, and a steel brush is preferred over a bronze bristle model, which isn't firm enough to strip lead. The best steel brushes are the spiral models, since they have the force to physically move lead. As far as solvents go, Shooter's Choice Lead Remover or Montana Xtreme Cowboy Blend work very well.

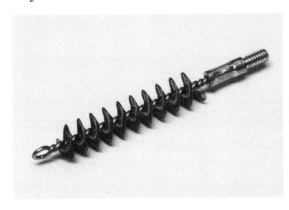

A spiral steel brush has the power to physically move lead, which bronze bristle brushes do not. If you shoot lead bullets you'll want a spiral brush.

With either, I wash the bore first with a powder solvent, let it sit a few minutes, run a brush through it as I would with the chemical process for jacketed bullets, and then dry-patch the bore. After that I wash the bore thoroughly with the lead solvent, and that sits for about ten minutes. The spiral brush is then run back and forth in the bore about fifteen times to strip out the lead that the solvent softened and raised. I repeat this process, and then push a couple of solvent-soaked patches one way through the bore with a jag. A couple of dry patches follow that. If a visual inspection shows a clean bore, I wash it with Corrosion X and leave it coated.

If the lead buildup is heavy, chemical cleaning may get it out if you're willing to spend enough time on it. I'm not, and in cases like these I generally reach for my Lewis Lead Remover. I only use it when the chemical method fails to get things as clean as I like, but it does wonders when leading is bad.

Since the bore has already been washed and brushed with lead solvent, then patched dry, I start by adding a little J-B

Cleaning Compound Paste to the brass patch and working it back and forth through the bore for a few minutes. The paste doesn't really help the brass patch move lead, but it does provide a bit of lubricant to make brushing easier. I'll then run a lead solvent patch through on a jag, dry-patch the bore, and see where I am. I'll repeat this until things look good, then wash the bore with solvent again and let it sit for ten minutes before dry-patching it out and oiling the bore.

The above procedure works well with plain lead. If gas checked bullets are used I will start with the same procedure, although it seldom takes as long. Once things look good, I patch in some copper solvent to see what, if any, copper fouling is present. When the patch shows me there is none, I remove the copper solvent with powder solvent, and dry and oil the bore. It only takes a few extra steps, but you don't want to overlook any potential copper build-up resulting from the gas check.

SAVING THE NEGLECTED BORE

Each of the above three cleaning procedures are designed to work with the specific type of projectile used, and they are definitely at their most effective when the bore has been properly broken in and regularly maintained. If the barrel hasn't been regularly maintained, some additional steps are in order.

If any of the above cleaning methods reveal that you have rust in the bore, it needs to be addressed immediately. Rust is a surface blemish that chemicals won't easily remove. Abrasive scrubbing is required and the most effective way to do that is to wash the bore with Kroil, and go right to one of the bore pastes. Scrub the bore for several minutes with the paste, then clean it out with Kroil. Dry-patch that and inspect the bore. If rust remains, repeat the Kroil and paste until it's gone. It's a matter of scrubbing with abrasives until you achieve the desired results.

If, however, you happen to be confronted with "The Bore from Hell," you'll need to go to a maximum-effort cleaning system. A badly neglected bore is going to look like a black sewer pipe and is not going to respond well to the chemical method at first. There is simply too much crud—of many different types— to be removed. The best way to start is to use the same abrasive/penetrating oil procedures used for cleaning a moly barrel. Start with the Kroil and let it sit for several minutes. Dry-patch that out and re-apply the Kroil. Repeat this several times, patch it out, and run Butch's Bore Shine. Let it sit a full ten minutes, and then see what a patch pushes out. If you are getting significant amounts of crud, stay with the Bore Shine for several more applications. If the debris is minimal, go to the J-B Bore Cleaning Compound. Stay with that until you can actually see some shine to the bore. It may take awhile.

Once the bore starts to look like a rifled barrel instead of a sewer pipe, you will have removed a lot of crud. There is likely going to be, however, some significant copper fouling still present. I will then dry-patch the bore and shift to copper solvents. I want the most aggressive I can find, and that means Shooter's Choice Copper Remover. Use as directed, repeatedly, until your patches show minimal copper washout.

My next step is to wash the bore thoroughly with Hoppe's #9 and let it sit overnight. The next morning, push a Hoppe's-soaked patch through on a jag and see what you have. The chances are good that you will have at least some black powder fouling and bluish copper washout. This is what was hiding in the tiniest microscopic cracks. If I see any, the barrel gets another Hoppe's wash and sits for a few hours before I check it again. Regardless of how those patches look, I will likely wash it for another overnight stay, and finish up the following day with another check, using copper solvent.

Some fouling can be so deeply embedded that it can take days to get out. If "the bore from hell" got that way from lead bullets, omit the moly cleaning procedures and start with the lead system. And get on the Lewis Lead Remover sooner; it's faster than the paste-and-oil system in getting a barrel down to some degree of shine. Once you get there, shift to the copper solvent and Hoppe's to finish up.

Even with this maximum effort system, you might not be able to bring the barrel back to an accurate shooting state. The neglect may have been too much and resulted in damage to the lands, grooves, throat, or crown. This should certainly be enough motivation to start your rifle barrel off right, and maintain it properly. If you don't love your barrel, it won't love you.

ACTION QUIRKS   **3**

Various action types can have different
but significant maintenance requirements.

Proper barrel cleaning is a relatively simple operation
that is influenced only by the type of projectile used.
When it comes to effectively maintaining the various
action types, however, things can get a little more complex.

The most important thing any shooter can do in that regard
is to be certain to retain the instruction manual that came with
the rifle. These often get tossed back into the box in which the

Many semi-autos,
and other repeating
rifles, are best
cleaned by disas-
sembling them.
Save the instruction
manual so you'll
know how to get
everything back
together.

gun came, and forgotten or even thrown out at a later date. That's not a good idea because proper cleaning can involve some degree of occasional disassembly on many action types, and the instruction manual will clearly show you how to do it.

Some disassembly procedures need to be done so infrequently that few shooters can remember them off the top of their head. Every gunsmith with whom I've ever spoken has plenty of funny stories regarding shooters bringing a gun into their shop in pieces and asking how to get it back together—often with a few small parts missing. That's not only a bit embarrassing, but it can get expensive. Making certain you have the manual can avoid that. If you lack the manual, contact the manufacturer and obtain one.

The manual will often spell out proper action maintenance requirements, in addition to providing instructions for the required disassembly and reassembly procedures. Detailed disassembly seldom has to be done in the course of routine cleaning, but every action type has a few things that should be checked on a regular basis.

BOLT ACTIONS

Bolt actions should be cleaned from the breech. Get the rifle in a vise or equivalent and remove the bolt. If you're using a bore guide you need only lay a couple of paper towels over the pistol grip area to keep everything neat and clean. If you're not using a bore guide, drop the magazine floor plate and open the interior so that you can slip a few crumpled-up paper towels into the magazine mortise. This will catch the solvent and debris that comes out of the bore with the rod, and keep crud out of your trigger assembly.

The trigger assembly does not require cleaning on a regular basis. The only time it really needs to be addressed is if the trigger starts feeling gritty, indicating that debris has gotten in there.

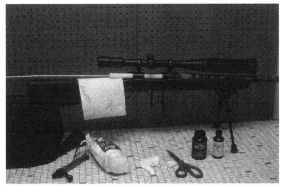

Bolt-action rifles should be cleaned from the breech. Add a bore guide and some paper towels, and it's a quick job with little mess. Note the barrel pointing downward. This is important with any action type since it keeps debris out of the action.

You can't clean most trigger assemblies with the action in the stock. When that part needs cleaning, pull the action from the stock and spray the assembly down with a quality degreaser. That normally blows the grit out. If it doesn't, do it again and work the exposed parts over with a toothbrush. Allow the degreaser to dry, and then lube the trigger assembly with a very light oil.

With the bolt out of the action, check the bolt face for any dings or cracks on the extractor claw, and for any burrs in the firing pin hole. A bit of powder solvent on a toothbrush will clean the bolt face properly. Disassembling, cleaning, and lubricating the bolt itself is seldom needed, but there are two occasions when it should be done.

The first is if you are going to be hunting in sub-zero weather. Extremely frigid temperatures can congeal old lubricating oil and powder fouling within the firing pin assembly and create misfires. The owner's manual will explain how to disassemble the bolt. It should then be cleaned with a degreaser (or carburetor spray), allowed to completely dry, and then re-lubricated with a very light coat of Corrosion X or FP-10, or with a dry lubricant like Sentry Solutions Tuf-Glide. Less lube is best here.

The second occasion is if the rifle has been completely submerged in water; especially saltwater. You can't let water sit inside a bolt housing. It will lead to rust that will freeze the firing mechanism, and the same applies to the trigger assembly.

One inspection that should be done every time your bolt gun is cleaned is a safety check. Some bolt action safeties work off the sear, and some off of the firing pin. But all can wear and fail to perform, which can create a very dangerous situation. The easiest way to check for a properly functioning safety is (with the gun unloaded, of course) to insert the bolt and close it to cock the action. Then, push the safety to the ON position and pull the trigger. Then, push the safety to the OFF position and do not pull the trigger. If the firing pin falls at any point during this cycle, your safety is malfunctioning: take the gun to a smith.

One should check the proper functioning of the safety after each cleaning.

While you have the gun set up for cleaning, this is an excellent time to put a screwdriver to every scope mount screw you can reach, and make sure they're tight. Those that aren't will come back to haunt you. And, if you have not removed the action from the stock during this cleaning session, check the tension on the action mounting screws.

SEMI-AUTOS

There are many different semi-auto actions on the market. Some must be cleaned from the muzzle, while others (like the AR-15 family) allow cleaning from the breech. If you just want a quick barrel scrub, all can be cleaned from the muzzle, and a muzzle guide is strongly recommended. Put the gun in a cradle, lock the bolt back, remove the magazine, pack some paper towels in the magazine well to catch crud, and clean the bore. This is a quick bore scrub and many high-power rifle competitors will do this between firing strings.

To truly clean any semi-auto, however, the gun needs to be disassembled in order to clean the gas system, bolt face, and trigger assembly. Failure to do so on a periodic basis will result in malfunctions.

Some types are easier to strip and clean than others. The AR-15, for example, is one of the most popular semi-autos made, with over fifteen different companies selling almost 125,000 annually. They are easy to detail clean—crack the rifle open, pull the bolt and bolt carrier, and everything is accessible. This is a direct gas system that blows gas back into the upper receiver to unlock the bolt. A lot of carbon gets built up in this area and the gas tube. A cleaning rod, patches, and powder solvent will remove it. One mistake some shooters make is to apply lubricant to the internal gas system. This is not good, because oil will carbonize under the heat and pressure of the propellant gases that are required to operate the action. Cleaning is all that is necessary on this gas system, as well as virtually all others.

Carbon will also build up on the bolt face and other operating parts. Break-Free Carbon Cutter is designed to remove this, and Hoppe's Elite also works. This needs to be removed or carbon can build to the point where parts will not properly mate.

Another popular semi-auto is the Ruger Mini-14 system. This rifle type's action needs to be removed from the stock in order to scrub carbon from the gas piston that mates with the forward end of the operating rod. Carbon buildup here can promote rust and make it very difficult to retract the operating rod to chamber or clear a round.

The trigger assembly on most semi-autos also needs more care. Depending upon the action type, they get bombarded with propellant gases and can collect a lot of debris. These are best removed from the gun, sprayed and brushed down, allowed to dry, and then lightly lubed.

If they are easily removable, the trigger group and bolt should be sprayed down and thoroughly cleaned on semi-auto actions.

One area that is often overlooked on semi-autos is the chamber itself. Normal barrel cleaning will not scrub it, and it must be clean and dry—no oil, either—in order for the rifle to feed and extract properly. A chamber brush is almost mandatory for proper maintenance. If you shoot an AR-15, Brownells offers a chamber brush specifically made for this action; it incorporates a raised section that also cleans the locking lug recess. It also works well on any other .223 caliber semi-auto, and is a worthy addition to the cleaning bench.

The bolt face should be inspected for proper functioning of extractor and firing pin, and scrubbed with a toothbrush.

A clean, dry chamber is very important, and on some guns with tight chambers it is critical. If you're having trouble with sticky feeding or extraction, and the gun is otherwise operating normally, check your chamber. The chances are good that's the culprit. Should you find any rust there, break out the bore paste and remove it.

You'll also want to check the bolt face to ascertain that the extractor is still in proper condition and that the firing pin portal has not been dinged or dented. Semi-autos operate rather vigorously and parts do wear or break.

The safety should be checked in the same manner one would with a bolt action, or any other action for that matter. A malfunctioning safety is dangerous on any firearm.

One component that is often ignored during routine maintenance is the magazine. They are usually pretty sturdy, but problems can arise. If the magazine has been subjected to a lot of dust and dirt, it can become gritty and not only fail to feed smoothly, but could transfer that grit to the rifle chamber. Magazine springs can also weaken with age and fail to properly position the cartridge to feed. A pitted or damaged magazine follower can cause rounds to hang up.

It is wise to periodically strip the magazine; your manual will show you how to do it (most are disassembled by depressing a button on the base plate, sliding it off, and removing the spring and follower). Magazines should be cleaned, but never lubricated. Cartridges will simply grab the oil and carry it to the chamber, where you don't want it, and the oil acts like a magnet to collect debris. If the follower is rough or pitted, it can quickly be polished with a Dremel tool, cotton polishing tip, and jeweler's rouge.

Lastly, don't forget to give a drop of oil to the various levers and buttons (magazine release, safety, bolt release, etc.) that comprise the operating controls.

PUMP ACTIONS

A pump action rifle is not much different than a semi-auto. The primary difference is that the energy for feeding and extraction is generated by the manual pressure on the forearm rather than the pressure generated by propellant gases.

They are still cleaned from the muzzle; a clean and dry chamber is important; magazines should be periodically inspected, and sometimes disassembled for cleaning; and the trigger group is best cleaned by removing (if your specific pump model allows it), spraying, and re-lubricating. The safety should routinely be checked, along with the bolt face, and don't forget to add a drop of oil to the various buttons and lever controls.

The action bars that allow the pump to work require lubricant, but are exposed to the elements where many lubes will grab dirt and debris. Grease is not recommended here. Instead, the best course is a dry lube, like Tuf-Glide, or Corrosion X or FP-10. Beyond that, routine maintenance is little different than that for semi-autos.

LEVER ACTIONS

All lever actions operate on the same basic principle: push the lever forward and it withdraws the bolt to extract the fired case, eject it, and place a new round onto the feed ramp; pull the lever back and the feed ramp rises while the bolt drives forward to shove the round into the chamber. Like pumps and semi-autos, these need to be cleaned from the muzzle unless they are one of the few "take down" lever guns on the market. And, as with other repeating rifles, a clean/dry chamber is a plus for reliable feeding.

Some lever guns use detachable magazines, although the majority use a tubular magazine under the barrel. The detachable-magazine models provide a bit more room in the action area where one can crumple some paper towels to keep the trigger group clean while the bore is being scrubbed. Tubular magazine guns don't have that space, and the easiest way to deal with them is to clean from the muzzle, and then spray the interior action areas down to remove whatever crud found its way in there.

Bolt faces should always be cleaned and inspected, but given the tight spaces on many lever guns this is best done with a small parts brush and spray.

Bolt faces on semi-autos, lever guns, and pumps can collect a lot of powder fouling and brass shavings from the cartridge. This area needs to be scrubbed clean.

Lever-action designs can vary quite a bit, but all of them depend upon a smoothly operating lever to drive the gun, and its pivot points should be properly lubed. With tubular magazines, the feed ramp must also have its bearing points lubed. Those guns using detachable magazines should have them stripped and cleaned periodically. The same applies to tubular magazines, but it is something that many shooters overlook.

A tubular magazine full of crud will transfer some of that junk to the cartridge, which then winds up in the interior action and even the chamber. With some models (especially rimfires or centerfires using lead bullets), lead or brass shavings can accumulate sufficiently in the tube to prevent the spring from properly feeding rounds. That's not good for reliability, but cleaning them is easy—the manual will show you how to remove the end cap and withdraw the spring and follower. Once that's done, run a powder solvent patch through the tube, spray the spring and follower with degreaser, let it dry, and reassemble. Like a detach-able magazine, these need no internal lubricant, nor is it desired.

SINGLE SHOTS

These are about as simple and bulletproof as you can make a rifle, and there are a wide variety of single-shot actions. This includes

Single-shot, break-top actions are the ultimate in simplicity when it comes to cleaning.

the break-top/interchangeable barrel models (like the H&R Top-per and Thompson Center guns), the various Rolling Block ac-tions, as well as the Winchester High and Low Walls, along with the Ruger #1. Routine maintenance on all is simple. Most can be cleaned from the breech, and should be if that is an option.

Some actions have a firing pin spring and some don't. On those that do, check to make sure there is free play in the spring. If the spring breaks or freezes up, it can hold the firing pin for-ward and fire the gun upon closing the action. While there, check the firing pin nose for chips or cracks.

On top break actions, check to see if there is any looseness between barrel and frame when the action is closed. If there is, it suggests worn locking lugs that need repair.

The only other area of concern is if the action feels loose in the stock. The through stock bolt can sometimes loosen a bit, but it can easily be tightened by removing the butt plate to access the bolt head.

RIMFIRES NEED EXTRA CARE

The lowly .22LR is a bit more complex than it looks.
Here's how to keep yours in top condition.

I f you're somebody who considers a rifle chambered for the .22 Long Rifle to be just a smaller version of a centerfire, you're partially right. They are smaller, kick less, are much cheaper to shoot, and can be great fun. But there are some noticeable differences that will affect accuracy, reliability, and the necessary maintenance. One is proper barrel care.

I'm a strong advocate of breaking in a centerfire rifle barrel. With the .22LR, I'm a bit more ambivalent. During my sojourn into small-bore competition some years ago I did break in the barrel of my match rifle. I had a feeling that it made a positive difference, but never really could prove it. That was the last .22LR barrel I ever broke in, and I've never regretted the decision to forego that expenditure in time.

It must be noted that my opinion is not shared by many expert small-bore shooters. A lot of them break in their barrels, and those to whom I've talked (whose opinion I respect) favor a fire lapping system. Brownell's has both the David Tubbs and NECO systems for rimfires. If you are engaged in competition, the time might be well-spent. But if you just want to pop tin cans, pine-cones, small game, and artificial targets, I can't honestly say the effort is worth it. There are other factors that will play a larger role in the accuracy you can achieve.

Serious rimfire competitors usually break in their .22LR barrels, but the author doesn't feel that it is necessary for all .22LR rifles.

Barrel cleaning is another area where I diverge from my established centerfire procedures. I don't use the multi-purpose cleaners very much in centerfires, but find them very adequate for the .22LR. The velocities generated by either lead or plated loads seldom exceed 1400 fps, and don't produce the deep fouling common at higher velocities. The cleaning chore involves less effort, and these products work well. With copper-plated loads, I don't feel bad if I wash the bore every 100 rounds or so, instead of the more frequent cleaning I would do with a centerfire model.

If I'm shooting lead loads, I don't clean the barrel very often. I really don't need to. My T/C Classic rifle loves CCI Green tag loads (.5-inch groups at 50 yards), and the accuracy doesn't de-crease over a couple hundred rounds. In addition, the external lubricant on lead bullets does a pretty good job of keeping the bore rust-free.

I would never be so casual with my centerfire rifles, but the .22LR is different. A laid-back approach isn't too bad. However, that doesn't apply when it comes to cleaning the action parts. Laid-back will not work here.

The .22LR is a very small cartridge, and the actions that house it are equally minuscule. There isn't much "space" there. Yet the .22LR is one of the dirtiest cartridges ever made. The extremely fast-burning powders that propel it leave a filthy residue everywhere within the action. The external lubrication on the lead loads adds its share, and you'll also shave a bit of lead bullet here and there as the rounds travel from the magazine to the chamber.

The end result is a wealth of crud flying around inside a very small space. It all finds a home within the action parts, and when combined with the lubricants on the action parts, you get a real mess. If this sludge isn't thoroughly cleaned, it will bring any semi-auto to a halt, and can get thick enough to make pumps and lever actions sluggish. In many cases it can even prevent the bolt from fully closing on the chambered cartridge, stop the extractor from removing a fired round from the chamber, or gum the trigger up so badly that it won't function. It requires an aggressive cleaning action, and my first step is to disassemble the gun to the largest extent possible (short of a full detail strip) and hose

The .22LR is an inherently dirty round that lives in a small space. Thorough action cleaning is critical for reliability.

the action down with carburetor cleaner. Then it gets careful attention with either a bronze parts brush or a toothbrush (for the trigger group).

A key area is the bolt face. This houses the rim-striking firing pin and the extractor. Even small amounts of sludge can

Powder, primer and shaved lead fouling can quickly accumulate in any .22LR action, and some degree of disassembly is needed to thoroughly clean it out.

prevent them from properly functioning. Another is the mouth of the chamber. This is where the extractor groove is, and it must be free of debris or the extractor can ride right over the chambered round and leave the fired case in the chamber. If your gun has a barrel feed ramp that guides the round into the chamber, it must also be free of debris or the nose of the bullet may hang up and fail to feed.

The chamber must be clean, dry, and free of oil or solvent in order to properly feed and extract. Dirty or wet chambers can result in sticking cases. This doesn't normally require a chamber brush (like a larger centerfire round would) because the chamber is virtually bore diameter. If your last cleaning step in the barrel is to twirl an oversize dry patch around the chamber for a while, you should be in good shape. If you are having feeding problems, check the chamber for rust or rough spots and remove them with a bore paste.

All of these parts work together to feed, fire and extract. If even one of them is dirty, things may not work as you intend.

The remaining steps are to clean up the bolt races and trigger group. You do not want any sludge, grunge, or visible debris anywhere in the action. It needs to be "bare metal" clean because even a small amount of sludge can cause performance problems sooner or later.

When you are dealing with a .22LR rifle, you can't get the internal action parts too clean. The larger spaces and tolerances of a centerfire rifle may let you get a bit sloppy, but the tiny .22 won't let you get away with that.

Regardless of how clean you get the action of your .22LR, don't count on it staying that way. When you consider the extremely small interior spaces as well as the inherently dirty .22LR round, it becomes clear that debris will build up as you fire it. At some point it will grunge up enough to inhibit proper feeding and extraction in semi-auto actions, and even some manual actions. Just how long that will take depends largely on how you lubricate the action.

Lubrication is obviously needed, but some products have an affinity for grabbing and holding firing debris; this eventually combines with the lubricant to form sludge and prevent proper functioning. Other products do not. Simply using the right lubricant can go a long way towards preventing malfunctions. This point was driven home to me a number of years ago during a test specifically intended to determine the most effective lubes for .22LR semi-autos.

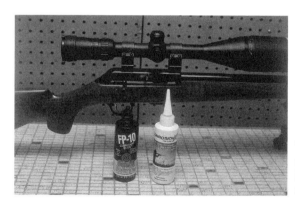

The right lubricant can go a long way in keeping your rimfire running smoothly.

I started with a Ruger MK II target pistol. This is a tubular receiver design, and does not expel debris as well as others. The gun was detail-stripped, cleaned, and then properly lubricated with one of the oils/greases in the test. Then, over a period of several days, I fired rounds through it—without additional cleaning or lubrication—until it started to experience failures to feed, extract, or seat the bolt, due to sludge build-up.

When that happened the gun was stripped, lubed with a different product, and fired again. It took months, but the results were interesting and a gun magazine was paying for the project anyway.

Any lubricant that had a grease base was lucky to make it 150–200 rounds before gunking up. These included some excellent lubricants that work very well in other applications. Light gun oils would stretch further, but none made it much beyond 350 rounds. They didn't trap as much debris as the grease-based products, but they eventually trapped enough to stop the gun.

When I got around to Corrosion X, the Ruger ran through a full 500-round brick without a stutter. I'm confident it would have run further, but didn't see any point in continuing. Shooter's Choice FP-10 was not included in those tests, but subsequent use has convinced me that its properties are similar to Corrosion X and it works well. Both of these have extremely light viscosity and form a polar bond with the metal. They provide the needed lubrication but don't collect the debris that forms sludge with oil- or grease-based lubricants. They not only extend reliable operation, but also make cleaning much easier.

Another way to keep your .22LR happy is to pay attention to the ammo you are using. Not all .22LR loads are created equal.

Manufacturing .22LR ammunition is a complex process. The parts are very small and the tooling needed to produce them is expensive and precise. Just imagine how difficult it is to properly pack just the right amount of priming compound inside the rim, let alone forming that small, precise case. And this is all accomplished with high-speed automated equipment.

Only the major ammo makers can afford the equipment to produce .22LR loads, and they also have to sell a lot of them to make a profit because the rounds are inexpensive (the market won't bear a high cost), with a very low profit margin. The bottom line is that once a production run is scheduled, and the tooling made, they are going to run that tooling as long as they can. Since tooling will wear, and produce minor dimension changes, over the course of a production run it's not surprising that the finished rounds will also have slight variations.

What generally occurs is that the first rounds in the run (before any significant tooling wear takes place) are slated for the premium or match product lines. These are labeled by lot number on the packaging. As the run continues and tooling wears, subsequent lots are packaged for less expensive product lines. As the tooling reaches the end of its useful life, you wind up with the 500-round boxes you can buy for a few bucks in discount stores. During the course of the entire run, bullet types and sometimes even powders are changed to produce the various product lines. But the tooling that makes the cases, packs the primers, and seats the bullets doesn't. This results in case dimensions that differ slightly as tooling wears over the course of a production run.

How this applies to rimfire shooters is fairly simple. Handloaders can resize a centerfire case to produce a perfect fit in their chamber and deliver peak accuracy. Rimfire shooters can't. They have to find the specific load that is the best fit for their chamber. This is old hat to smallbore rifle competitors, and they will routinely test different lots from a production run to find the most accurate in their individual rifle—and then buy as much of that specific lot number as they can. If your load shoots one-inch and the competitor's load will do a half-inch, you're going to lose.

This was actually a problem for our Olympic shooters during the days when the British firm of Eley was the preeminent producer of world-class .22LR match ammo. The European shooters usually beat our guys and gals to the best lots, and we got the dregs. That prompted Federal Cartridge Company to do some extensive research into the subject and produce a match load with which our shooters could win. This also explains why some .22LR loads will shoot more accurately in your rifle than others—the dimensions of those loads are a better fit for your chamber. It can also explain why some rounds will feed more reliably than others, especially if you have purchased a rifle with a "Match Chamber." A friend of mine who used to run a commercial hunting operation in Central Florida is a good example.

He did a lot of pest control work with a .22LR and wanted the best, so he had a Ruger 10/22 tuned and fitted with a Match barrel. Unfortunately, I could never break him of the habit of buying his bullets by the bucket at Wal-Mart. He got tired of marginal accuracy and more than a few jams and couldn't figure out why his "Match" rifle was performing so poorly.

It's not hard to figure. A Match-cut chamber is minimum dimension. It's specifically cut to function superbly with match-grade loads—the first ones off the line when cartridge specs are tight. The loads at the end of the run aren't, and can produce chambering problems in these guns. At the least, they seldom shoot well because you are crunching a case that may be just a touch oversized into the chamber. He eventually sold that gun and got an inexpensive lever action. It shot the cheap stuff as well as he needed, and it always worked. Having a match-grade

Achieving peak accuracy from your .22LR is sometimes no more complicated than finding the specific load it likes best.

.22LR is only a benefit if you are going to feed it match-grade ammo, and many shooters don't need to go that route.

The bottom line is this: if you find a particular load that your .22LR loves, use it. Don't automatically assume that a "bucket o' bullets" will produce the same results. All .22LR rounds are not created equal. While the .22LR is the most common rimfire, it's not the only one, and the others are a bit different in their maintenance requirements. If you're shooting a .17 HMR, .17 Mach2, or the .22 WMR you are technically shooting a rimfire round, since that is the priming system used. But unlike the .22LR, chamber dimensions are very standard. In the case of the .17 calibers, they are so new that essentially all dimensions came from the Hornady engineers and are industry standard. Some lot-to-lot variations can occur, but the problem is insignificant when compared to the .22LR.

In that respect they are different, but there are still some similarities. These also use quick-burning powders that are dirtier than those used in centerfire guns, and given the small spaces available within the action, you will build up more powder fouling than you'll get with the Big Boys (although not as much as with lead bullets in a .22LR). In that regard, the same careful action-cleaning and lubrication procedures used on the .22 LR are certainly in order here.

The biggest difference, however, is how your all-important barrel views these loads. They may be rimfire-primed, but as far as your barrel is concerned they are no different than copper-jacketed centerfire rounds. Depending upon the caliber and load, lighting off one of these rimfires will send a copper-clad slug down the barrel at velocities ranging from 1800 fps to 2600 fps. That's well within the same velocity range as a number of popular centerfire loads, including the .308 Win, .30–30, 7x57, and others. That produces the same type of copper bore fouling, and when you are dealing with a minuscule bore diameter like the

.17s, it doesn't take much to degrade accuracy. These guns need to be cleaned with the same chemical method used for copper-jacketed centerfire loads, and sometimes even a bit more often.

The .22LR rounds at left and center, and the .22 WMR load at right are all rimfires. But the WMR requires more attention to barrel care.

In my opinion, it is just as important to properly break these barrels in, like a careful shooter would do with a centerfire. In regards to what happens in the bore, there is virtually no difference between the two. The smoother the bore and throat, the less fouling will build, and the longer that barrel will deliver peak accuracy. Breaking in one of these barrels is done in exactly the same manner as outlined in Chapter 2 for breaking in a centerfire barrel with copper-jacketed loads.

One maintenance chore that is often overlooked with the .17s and the .22 WMR is applying a bore preservative if the gun is going to be laid up for a few months. A lot of shooters don't, and it's easy to understand why. For years, shooters have been taught that you don't need to oil the bore of a .22LR that's shooting lead bullets because the external lubricant on the bullet will do it for you. That has somehow been transposed to "rimfires" in general, but it is hardly the case. There is no external lube on copper-clad bullets. And even if the bore is scrubbed down to bare metal before the rifle is stored at the end of the season, it still needs a bore preservative, just like any centerfire rifle.

It's even more important on these, because the small bore diameter doesn't provide any airflow to displace atmospheric moisture. Add even a little atmospheric moisture to a .17 caliber bore and there is nowhere for it to go. You might get enough airflow through a .30 caliber bore to keep moisture from forming a surface tension, but not in a .17 tube. There just isn't enough space.

When one of these guns is about to go back into the gun rack until next season, first take the time to clean the bore thoroughly and apply a quality bore preservation like Corrosion X, FP-10 or one of the rust-preventative sprays. The bore will be nice and shiny when you break it out the next season. If you don't, you're taking your chances.

Rimfires are fun, economical, and very useful little rifles. But they do require some extra care if you want to keep them operating at their peak.

STOCK TIPS 5

Stocks are sturdy,
but they do require care.

The rifle's stock performs two basic functions. It holds all the mechanical action parts in their proper place so they can function as intended, and it gives the shooter something to hang onto while he shoots.

That's a rather simple job description, and it doesn't take a delicate mechanism to perform it. As a result, the stock is a pretty robust part of the rifle and it generally takes a catastrophic failure to render one inoperable. But they are not bulletproof, and there are a few things that need to be routinely done to them, along with a few things that can occasionally go wrong and require minor repairs. Just which will affect you depends largely upon what your stock is made of.

ROUTINE MAINTENANCE

The most common synthetic stocks are constructed by laying fiberglass over a core material that may be foam, Kevlar-reinforced foam, or some other synthetic material. They are virtually imper-vious to moisture and warping. They may be of any color or com-bination of color, and the coloring is normally incorporated within the external fiberglass, or in some cases painted onto the finished stock.

Laminated stocks are made in much the same way as ply-wood. Sheets of wood, of varying thickness, are laid onto each other with the grain structure running in the opposite direction of the adjacent sheets. These separate sheets are epoxy-coated and then compressed and bonded to each other under heat and pressure. The resulting block of wood can then be carved into a rifle stock. They are very resistant—although not impervious—to moisture and seldom warp. They are much stronger (as well as heavier) than a traditional wood stock.

The traditional wood stock is just that—a solid blank of walnut, maple, birch or other hardwood that is carved into a stock. The grain structure invariably runs in one direction and these stocks can warp due to accumulated moisture (wood is hygro-scopic and the pores will hold moisture) or as a result of sudden extreme temperature changes.

Traditional solid wood stocks begin life as a blank, with the grain running in one direction. They need more moisture protection than other stock materials.

Regardless of the type of stock you have, moisture is an enemy, and routine maintenance is required to combat it. Syn-thetic stocks won't absorb moisture, but they will collect it. Water, be it from a good soaking in the rain or simply due to atmospheric moisture, will creep into the barrel channel and action bedding area. Once there it has nowhere to go other than to the metal on the barrel and action surfaces. It stays trapped between the fiberglass and the metal, which leads to rust.

Those opting for synthetic stocks should periodically remove the action from the stock and apply a light coat of rust-preventative anywhere metal contacts the stock. If you get caught in a rainstorm, pull the action and dry everything off before applying a preservative. This will keep the hidden parts of your rifle from rusting.

The same routine maintenance is also required on a wood stock (solid or laminated), but you need to go one step further. The external portions of any wood stock will have some type of finish applied that will help repel moisture. The internal stock areas almost never do. The barrel channel, magazine mortise, areas under barrel bands and other non-visible spots where metal contacts the stock are usually rough-cut, unfinished wood.

Unfinished wood is a moisture magnet. The wood pores will absorb moisture and swell, but once the moisture evaporates the pores dry out and contract. This constant expansion and contraction can lead to rotting or cracking. And, while the wood pores are moisture filled they can promote rust when in contact with metal.

You can prevent this on any wood stock by routinely applying a light coat of boiled linseed oil (available at most quality hardware stores) to all internal areas of the stock. Remove the action from the stock, dab some linseed oil on a cloth or your fingers, rub it into the unfinished wood, let it sit for fifteen minutes, and wipe the excess off with a cloth. Do this two or three times a year and your wood stock will last a lot longer. The linseed oil helps fill pores (preventing expansion and contraction) while repelling moisture.

While you have the action removed from the stock, this is an excellent time to check for rust or touch up scratches or worn

The interior areas of a wood stock are unfinished wood. Periodic applications of boiled linseed oil will seal them from moisture.

bluing. There are several cold bluing solutions on the market. Birchwood Casey Perma Blue is one of the simplest. The procedure involves cleaning the small section to be re-blued with a degreaser or Birchwood Casey Blue and Rust Remover, removing any surface rust with a fine grade of steel wool, and then swabbing on a bit of the Perma Blue. Let it sit for a few minutes and then wipe it down with a water-dampened cloth. Repeat this until you get the desired degree of bluing. The directions on the product are simple, it takes little time, and it will help prevent worn bluing areas from rusting.

MINOR REPAIRS

While moisture is something against which one must always be on guard, there are other things that can happen to your stock due to age and wear that require minor repairs. One is a loose sling swivel stud. Any that are screwed directly into a wood or synthetic stock (without a backing nut inside the stock) can loosen over time. Wood can shrink with age, and synthetic stocks can compress under stress. The end result is that sling studs can become loose.

With a wood stock the simplest "quick fix" is to break off a couple of small pieces of wooden match shaft, insert them into the stud hole, and then screw the stud back in place. They will fill the hole that has widened in the wood. A few wraps of plumber's tape over the threads on the stud will accomplish the same thing.

A quick fix for loose sling swivel studs can be had by stuffing a few matchstick shafts into the screw hole and re-inserting the stud.

Another option is to coat the interior of the stud hole with Brownells Acraglass, let that set for a few minutes, coat the screw thoroughly with the Release Agent (included with the Acraglass kit), and then insert the screw until the glass dries. Acraglass is a stock bedding epoxy and it will make a "new" set of threads. But—and this in important—make certain the Release Agent is used on all parts of the stud that will contact the Acraglass or you will have made a permanent weld between the stud and stock. This will work with either wood or synthetic stocks, and is the preferred method for the latter.

Another screw problem (that occurs more often in synthetic stocks) is the screw holes that allow the action screws to connect with the action parts, through the stock, expanding or becoming cracked. As mentioned earlier, a synthetic stock is nothing more than a fiberglass outer shell laid over a filled foam. The action bedding screw holes take a lot of stress due to recoil, and the fiberglass/foam is not strong enough to take it. The result is that virtually all synthetic stocks have these holes lined with a stronger third material, generally some form of epoxy.

Over time, particularly with hotter calibers, recoil will cause stress cracks in this epoxy lining and the hole can widen, increasing the potential for trouble. The solution for that is to remove the action from the stock: drill out the old epoxy with a slightly oversize drill (this is just a hole, there are no threads involved), coat the interior of the action screw hole with Acraglas, apply Release Agent to the action screw and any internal parts of the metal action that the glass might contact, and then screw it back together until it dries. Remove the screw, clean up any excess epoxy with a Dremel Tool or file, and the hole is restored to the original factory dimensions. This will work on either front or rear action holes, although the front hole is usually where the problem occurs.

EXTERNAL COSMETICS

Many rifles have some form of checkering on the pistol grip and forearm. Since this is where the shooter holds the gun, it's not surprising that the checkering soon gets gummed up with mud, oil, blood, grease, shed skin particles, and just plain gunk. Cleaning that out isn't difficult, but you need to remember one thing—checkering is unfinished wood. Regardless of whether it is cut or impressed, the checkering is done after the stock has been finished. That checkering, which broke through the finish no matter how it was accomplished, is easy to clean, but you don't want to use harsh chemicals.

A light solution of soap and water, and a clean toothbrush (you don't want to scrub it with the one you've been using to clean powder fouling) are recommended. There are a number of solutions that will work, but my good friend Jack Mitchell (who is an expert on stock work) recommends Simple Green's All Purpose Cleaner. Apply some directly to the toothbrush and scrub away. This is available many places (I get mine at Home Depot), and makes short work of caked-on crud. The directions on the bottle say don't use it on unfinished wood, but I have had good results on stock checkering.

A clean toothbrush and Simple Green cleaner will quickly clean checkering on any stock.

Once the checkering is cleaned, it needs some protection, but heavy waxes and other finishes often attract too much debris and remain tacky. Mitchell recommends a very light coat of Scott's Liquid Gold. This is readily absorbed into the wood (which prevents moisture accumulation) and dries hard to the touch. This can be sprayed on (in the spray formulation) or brushed on lightly with a toothbrush, if you get the liquid version. Either works well.

Minor dings and dents in a synthetic stock are easy to repair. Clean out any debris with a cotton swab and alcohol, mix

Dings and gouges in a synthetic stock can be quickly repaired with a two-part epoxy, and paint can be mixed with the epoxy to match the original stock color.

a two-part epoxy, and fill the dent. Level it off with a flat tool like a Popsicle stick, and when it dries you can sand off any excess. This will be a clear filler, but if you want to match the stock color you can mix the appropriate color paint right in with the epoxy. Any paint will work, since it's encapsulated within the epoxy filler.

Minor dents on wood stocks can usually be raised by soaking a towel with water, laying it over the dent, and applying a steam iron to the towel. It may take several applications, but it gets the minor ones raised.

A major gouge, where wood fibers are actually broken, is another matter. You can raise it some with the towel/iron, but seldom enough. Filling it with epoxy or wood putty is usually the only option. If the gouge is severe, and in a recoil stress area, a gunsmith is needed. Home repairs here are not recommended for safety reasons: if that repair lets go under recoil, you could be injured.

If the finish on a wood stock is worn away and bare wood is exposed, it can be patched to protect the wood. Oil finishes are the easiest to repair. You first need to determine what type of oil was used on the stock, and the maker can often provide that information. It will invariably be either Birchwood Casey's Tru-Oil, Tung Oil (one product available from Brownells is made by Old

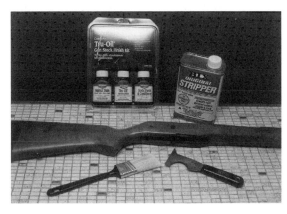

Birchwood Casey's Tru-Oil refinishing kit is a convenient way to dress up an old stock.

Masters), or WATCO Danish Oil (often just called Danish Oil) and all are available over the counter.

Once you have the proper oil, sand the damaged area with 220-grit sandpaper, clean that up with a tack cloth (a cotton rag dampened with mineral spirits or rubbing alcohol works fine), apply a sanding sealer like Minwax Sanding Sealer and let that dry overnight. The next day, sand that with 220-grit, tack cloth it, let it dry, and rub in one thin coat of oil. Let that sit overnight and repeat the procedure until you have three coats of oil. It should match the original finish very well.

With varnish or polyurethane finishes (commonly called "plastic finishes") you will not likely be able to match the patch to the rest of the finish. This is especially true with plastic finishes because the factories use urethane products that are not available to the consumer. In the case of a varnish finish, you can just clean the area, rough it up with 220-grit sandpaper, and brush on some varnish. The wood will be protected, even if the cosmetics aren't.

With a plastic finish, clean the area, rough it up with 220-grit, extend that for about one-half inch around the blemish, and fill it with Minwax Wipe On Poly. When that dries, sand it down with 220-grit. This will protect the wood, but the patch will be glaringly obvious. You can minimize that by then rubbing the patch down with automotive rubbing compound, followed by automotive polishing compound, and finishing with glazing compound. All are available at most auto parts stores. This will get you as close to a match as possible, but the patched area will still show what is called "orange peel" (high spots, low spots, and some sanding dust) at certain angles and light conditions.

If protection is the goal and cosmetics unimportant, these will work with varnish and plastic finishes. If cosmetics count, you might want to ask yourself . . .

SHOULD YOU REFINISH?

Refinishing a stock is not difficult, but it is time-consuming. And the results you get will largely depend on the time you put into the project. There is no quick way to completely refinish a stock and produce an acceptable job. A Ruger Mini-14 stock refinishing I recently completed is a good example.

This was an inexpensive hardwood stock with a varnish finish, and since the color was very light (and I used it as a "calling gun" for coyotes) I had covered the stock with camo tape to reduce glare. When I decided to remove the tape after a decade, it left an adhesive residue. In the course of removing that with mineral spirits, some of the varnish finish was also removed. I didn't care for the color—or the varnish finish—anyway, so this was a good time to transform it into a dark-walnut-stained, oil-finished, stock.

The first step was to remove the stock from the action, and remove the recoil pad and sling swivel stud from the butt. They get in the way, and paint strippers can damage the recoil pad. (This stock had no checkering. If it had, I would have carefully cut masking tape and covered the checkering. When refinishing a stock you don't want to touch the checkering. Don't strip it, sand it, stain it, or finish it. Cover it with tape and leave it as is through the entire refinishing process unless you intend to completely remove it and re-cut the checkering.)

The next step was to strip the old finish from the stock. Chemical finish strippers are the best bet, and they work well on varnish, paint, lacquer or the urethane (plastic) finishes. There are different formulations available (from Home Depot, etc.), depending on the finish to be removed. I used Bix Stripper for this varnish finish. This must be done in a well-ventilated area (outside is strongly recommended), and you definitely should wear eye protection and chemically resistant gloves.

This product is brushed on, and allowed to set while it dissolves and raises the old finish. That is then removed with a putty knife or plastic scraper. Don't try to do the whole stock at once. Work a quarter or half at a time so you have something to hang onto while you scrape. Once the whole stock was stripped, I rubbed it down with water and a light steel wool, then hung it to dry overnight in a clean and breeze-free room. The easiest way to hang it is to reinstall a sling swivel stud and make a hanging bracket from a coat hanger that goes through the stud hole.

There were a few dings and dents in the stock, and these were raised with a wet towel and a steam iron. After that it was rough-sanded with 80-grit sandpaper, followed by 150-grit, and finish-sanded with 220-grit. This takes time, but the final finish depends a lot on the quality of the sanding job. You don't want to cut corners here, because every little nick you miss is going to stand out brilliantly when the final finish is complete. Between each sanding the stock was "tack clothed" (thoroughly wiped down to remove sanding dust) with a cotton rag moistened with mineral spirits, and after the final sanding and tack cloth I hung it up overnight again.

The next step was the stain, and I used Birchwood Casey water-based Walnut Stain. This is a concentrate that you mix with water to get the degree of color you want. A few trial tests on the forearm got the mixture where I wanted it, and the entire stock was coated with a brush. This stain dries darker than it appears when wet, so it's a good idea to take it slow and work up one small section, letting it dry for a couple of hours to determine the exact shade you want, before you stain the entire stock. The coat hanger in the swivel stud gives you something to hang onto when doing a full stock. That was hung to dry overnight.

The following day the stock was ready for finishing. Had I wanted to use a polyurethane plastic finish (like Minwax Wipe On Poly), I could have started applying the finish right then. Since I wanted an oil finish, however, I applied a coat of Minwax

Sanding Sealer and hung that to dry overnight. The sealer is needed with oil.

By now, the "hanging overnight" part is probably getting a bit old, but it's necessary. The biggest mistake made in refinishing a stock is not allowing each operation/coating to completely dry, and cure, between applications. If a new coat is applied over something that isn't fully dried, the previous coat will not fully dry. The stock will stay tacky for a long time and fingerprints will result from handling.

Once the sanding sealer was dry, it got a rubdown with 220-grit, tack-clothed with mineral spirits, and hung to dry again.

There are several oil finishes available. Birchwood Casey makes a very convenient kit for its Tru Oil finish, but I wanted to use Tung Oil so I opted for Formby's Tung Oil Finish. Like everything else used in this project, Home Depot carries it. The key to a quality tung oil finish is to apply one very thin coat at a time, rubbing it thoroughly into the wood just like you were waxing a vintage automobile, and then allowing it to thoroughly dry before the next coat. The first coat you put on should be light enough to not even look like you coated it. Do the entire stock at one time, and hang it to dry. Formby's says it should take twelve hours, but I give it a minimum of 24 hours. I hate a tacky oil finish.

Once that is dry, buff it lightly with a fine steel wool pad (Formby's, and others, make a steel wool refinishing pad for this

Refinishing a stock with Tung Oil is a simple, yet lengthy, process.

purpose), wipe it down with a lint-free cloth, apply a second thin coat and hang it up to dry. Repeat this until you have four coats on the stock.

If you've taken your time, properly prepped the wood, and allowed everything to thoroughly dry, you will have a beautiful finish—one that's easy to keep looking good.

Professional stock finishers know that you get no better finish than the time you put into it. This is not a job that can be rushed.

CURING THE WACKY RIFLE

6

Accuracy problems can crop up unexpectedly,
but can often be fixed quickly with a
systematic approach.

If this hasn't happened to you yet, rest assured that at some point it probably will.

Hunting season approaches, so you dig your favorite deer rifle out of the closet and head to the range to check the sights. The first round isn't where you expect it to be, the second isn't very close to the first, and the third wanders further still. Subsequent groups continue to look pretty bad.

Congratulations, your rifle has just gone "wacky" on you. It's not uncommon, even though the gun may have been shooting tight and on the mark when you put it up last year. If this happens at home, before the hunt, count yourself as somewhat fortunate. It could happen on the hunt itself, especially if the rifle has gone through a lengthy transport to get there. Regardless of where it happens, you have a tool that is not doing the job and needs to be fixed.

A "wacky" rifle is different than a "broken" rifle. The former appears to be functioning properly but won't shoot where it looks and the groups are terrible. The latter is obviously malfunctioning due to a broken part within the action mechanism. The broken gun needs the services of a gunsmith; the wacky rifle often doesn't. Sometimes the fix can be surprisingly quick and simple, while other solutions may be a bit more complex. But all but the most extreme are within the capabilities of the shooter.

Determining which fix is needed is best accomplished with a systematic approach that looks at each part of the overall accuracy equation, and either confirms that part as the problem or eliminates it from consideration.

The first step is to make certain it's the gun and not the shooter.

IS IT YOU?

This may sound elementary, but it's often overlooked. The only way to truly determine the accuracy capability of a rifle and particular load is to group-test it. Once you know that Load A is capable of consistent three-shot groups of 1.5 inches at 100 yards—and to point of aim—you have a base line for performance.

Getting an accurate base line requires that as much human element as possible be removed from the group firing process, and that mandates a solid rest. The ideal rest is one that allows you to move the sights to a precise point on the target, remove your hands from the gun, and have the sights stay at (or at least real close) to that spot. Once that is accomplished, the only human element remaining is the shooter's grip on the gun and the trigger press.

Getting that degree of stability isn't possible by just putting any object under the forearm and letting the butt wobble with the shooter. The resulting groups will depend upon how sharp the shooter is that day, and not necessarily on how well the gun and load will perform. And if some of the multiple-bags-under-the-

Using a solid rest is important in determining the health of your rifle. If the perch is shaky, you can't count on the groups being an accurate indicator of what the gun can do.

forearm-with-the-shooter-sitting-bolt-upright-and-the-butt-stock-wobbling-way-out-in-space systems I have seen at public ranges are any indication, that shooter had better be dead-on sharp if anything resembling a group is going to be produced. Even then, you can't count on the accuracy of that data. The only worthwhile rifle performance data is that which can be replicated during subsequent group tests.

A single bag under the forearm is not the best way to accomplish that. But if the bag is a low one that keeps the gun down low to the bench, and the shooter gets down tight to the rifle, and then moves the off-hand under the butt to provide some degree of rear support, a skilled shooter can still achieve acceptable results with it.

A two-piece bag system is more effective if you can plump the rear bag up enough to offer full hands-off support. An alternative is a short bipod on the forearm and a rear bag under the butt. This can work quite well if the shooter keeps one thing in mind: if you place the bipod on a hard, unyielding surface (like a shooting bench or the hood of your pickup truck), it's not uncommon for some rifles to show vertical stringing. This is because the rifle will recoil away from a hard surface (which the bipod is functionally putting it in direct contact with), and any minor variations in the grip pressure of the shooter will alter the degree of recoil in the rifle for different shots. Vertical stringing will result. The solution is to fold a soft cloth towel and place it under the bipod. That creates a yielding surface and eliminates vertical stringing.

Bipods are handy in the field, but if they are placed on a hard surface they can create some degree of vertical stringing.

In my opinion, the most effective rest is a large single bag, like the Hughes Ballistic Shooting Bag I use. This is a long bag that fully supports the forearm of the rifle and holds the entire gun in one spot. A base tray supports the bag and has an adjustment for elevation. By shifting the tray right or left, and using the elevation wheel, you can put the crosshairs on the target and have them stay there when you remove your hands from the gun. It's about as stable as you can make a portable rest. The only way to ruin the shot is via a sloppy trigger press.

With a proper rest you can group-test a number of loads and determine the gun's capabilities with each. Save those targets, and note the specific load and the date. That becomes your performance base line and can tell you when you rifle is going wacky—sometimes even before it hits full wacky. This is one of the most beneficial things you can do to monitor the health of your rifle, because if you don't know when it's doing well, it's hard to determine when it's doing poorly.

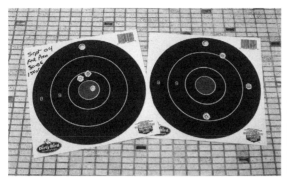

Keeping reference targets for proven loads (left) can help you determine if your rifle is mis-behaving (right).

When group testing to obtain base-line data, don't rush. Fire a three-round group and let the gun cool for a few minutes before the next group. In extremely hot weather, ten minutes is not too long to let the barrel cool. A hot barrel seldom delivers the same accuracy as a cold one and may experience a slight point-of-impact shift. If you're going to take the time to test fire and sight in, take the time to get accurate data.

HOW'S YOUR AMMO?

If you have previous performance data, a solid rest, and are con-fident that each shot was properly delivered, yet the groups are far larger than normal, the first step in figuring out where the problem lays is to check your ammunition. Are you using loads you have found worked well in the past? If you know Loads A, B, and C all shoot about 1.5 inches and you are using a new load that shoots 2.5 inches, it's not yet time to blame the rifle. Your gun may not like that load and if you haven't group tested it in the past you won't know. Try some loads you have used in the past, and have data on, before digging into the rifle. Serious rifle-men usually have one load that has consistently performed well and is used as their "reference load." If the reference load shoots like it always does, the rifle isn't the problem.

Did you wind up with some moly-coated loads when all you have shot in the gun are plain-jacketed slugs? This happens more often than some might suppose, and it's easy to do. Consider the following likely scenario: the casual hunter (who may not fire more than a box of ammo a year and may not be particularly knowledgeable on loads) heads down to the local bullet emporium to get some ammo for the upcoming season. The counter salesman starts touting the performance of this year's crop of new loads, and how much better they are than last year's. His description of their degree of increased performance may often depend on how big an order he placed for them and how many he has in stock. The salesman may mention they are moly coated, but neither he nor the hunter may really understand what that means. The loads are "new" so they must be better. The hunter buys a couple of boxes, heads to the range to sight in, and starts feeding them through his rifle—which has never shot moly, and has copper fouling in the barrel. Not only are groups miserable, but may not even be close to the point of aim. The hunter is at a loss to explain it, and may even be contemplating an in-depth "discussion" of their performance with the salesman who recommended them . . . especially if the salesman is smaller than he is.

Moly-coated bullets (right) will not shoot accurately unless the barrel has been deep cleaned and prepped for them. If your groups go south, check your ammo.

This situation, however, is easily explained and not unexpected. Moly-coated bullets generally exhibit poor accuracy in any barrel where copper jacketed fouling is present. And, given the different dwell time in the barrel, they seldom shoot to the same point of aim as jacketed loads. This was explained in more detail in Chapter 2, but there are three things the shooter can do to correct this fairly quickly.

The first is to go back to the jacketed loads that worked well in the past. You don't even need to clean any moly fouling out, because the jacketed slugs will do it for you. Moly won't shoot accurately in a copper-fouled barrel, but jacketed bullets will shoot in a moly-fouled barrel.

The second solution is to properly prep the barrel for moly as detailed in Chapter 2: scrub it down to bare metal, fire ten moly rounds to season it, and then sight in to see how the new loads do.

The third solution might be considered a "dire straits improvisation," but it can occur. In fact, it happened to me about a dozen years ago on a prairie dog hunt. A major ammo company invited some writers out West to pop prairie dogs with their loads, and I hauled along my long-range .243 Model 70 with the intent of wringing it out on 400-yard-plus dogs. I was shooting jacketed bullets through it at the time and several of this company's loads were real tack drivers. I called them, told them what loads shot best, and was assured they would be there.

After a lengthy flight we gathered at the host motel, sorted out our gear, and had a pleasant dinner that included an adequate number of adult beverages. It was my kind of place and I was in a great mood.

The following morning we wandered about twenty miles out of town to a sight-in range. Once I got the Model 70 set up on bags, I went to the supply van to get the loads of which I'd been assured. They weren't there. Among all the cases of ammo, the only .243 loads were "new" moly-coated slugs. I tried a few, and my half-inch rifle turned into a 2.5 inch gun.

Prior to leaving home I'd zeroed the gun with the specified jacketed loads and run a half-dozen fouling shots through it. Cleaning and seasoning would have worked to change to moly, but my cleaning gear was 20 miles behind me at the motel. I was about to get moderately irked (some of the participants at the sight-in session may remember my response in less charitable terms) when I recalled a piece of advice from an experienced moly shooter, to the following effect: if you have copper fouling in the bore and have to shoot moly without being able to scrub and season it, just start pounding moly bullets through it. Sooner or later the moly will coat the copper and the gun will start to shoot.

I'd never tried that. But seeing as how I had no choice, and there were cases of ammo on hand, this seemed as good a time as any to test the theory. Forty rounds, and an hour later, the gun started to settle down. About fifteen rounds after that it was tossing nice little sub-half-inch clusters, and a few clicks on the scope brought them to point of aim.

It turned out to be a great shoot, and I did become a fan of moly on that trip. My last shot of the hunt, after about 300 moly rounds without cleaning the barrel, smoked a prairie dog at a laser-measured 553 yards.

Given the cost of factory moly coated loads, however, I wouldn't recommend this procedure over the other two options. But, what the heck, I had no choice, the ammo was free, and it did work.

ARE YOUR SIGHTS LOOKING WHERE YOU ARE?

If checking your ammo doesn't solve the problem, the next step is to check the sights.

Sights that are shifting under recoil, and looking at a different spot on the target each shot, are the most common cause of a wacky rifle, and sometimes the easiest to fix. It's often nothing more than a loose screw or two, and tightening it up cures the problem.

Iron sights are largely bullet proof. If the front sight looks like it's supposed to, and doesn't wiggle in your fingers, it's good to go. Wiggle the rear sight as well, it could be loose in its base, and tightening the mounting screws cures that. Some models of adjustable iron sights use springs to maintain the blade position, and these can occasionally weaken or break. The recoil from each shot then shifts the blade and groups open. If the blade wiggles just a touch, that's normal. If it wobbles around severely under pressure, it needs to be checked by a competent gunsmith. You may need a new rear sight, although some models can be repaired with new springs.

Scope systems are far more complex. Most will utilize a separate base plate that screws to the receiver, which holds the rings that are screwed around the scope, via screws that mate the rings and base. That's a lot of screws and if one or more of them loosen, recoil can shift the scope in the same manner as a broken iron sight. If you grip the scope and it wiggles at all, that's a strong indication of a screw problem, and it's time to check every one of them. Even if it appears to be solid, check them anyway. It

Loose scope-mount screws can result in poor accuracy, but tightening them back down will fix it. The Weaver system, shown here, is one of the quicker mount systems to correct.

doesn't take much loosening of any screw to cause the scope to shift to some degree.

Some mounts are less susceptible to problems than others, and much easier to fix. The most trouble-free, in my opinion, are the integral ring mounts like the Sako, Ruger or CZ systems. There are two rings on the scope that become a one-piece unit with the scope, and mate directly to grooves on the receiver via one big screw on each ring. Each screw on the entire mount system is easily accessible without removing the scope from the rings or the rifle. If one or more loosens (the screws securing the scope to the receiver are usually the culprits here), they are quick to tighten up and it seldom results in a point-of-impact shift.

Another excellent system is the Weaver type. Base plates screw to the receiver, and the ringed scope mounts to them via dovetailed cross bolts. Once the scope is properly mounted in the rings, the scope and rings essentially becomes one unit. If the base plate screws loosen (that's the usually culprit with this system) you can pop the scope/rings off, quickly tighten the base plate, and put the scope back on with little, if any, change in zero. These are the two scope mounting systems I would prefer on any rifle, or scope-sighted handgun. They're simple, sturdy, and very quick to check and fix.

Other scope mounting systems are not nearly as much fun. There's no point in naming them, but any scope mounting system that requires removal of the scope from the rings in order to reach the base plate screws is something I avoid. There is virtually no way you can do that, reinstall the scope, and not have to completely re-sight the rifle. And base plate screws are usually the ones that loosen and need periodic checking.

Even less fun are those mounts that incorporate windage screws on each side of the rear rings. These function by opposing each other under pressure. To use them to adjust windage you loosen one, tighten the opposing screw to physically move the scope, and then tighten the first screw to lock it in. These screws are notorious for loosening on their own. It's not a question of whether they will or not; it's merely a matter of when. And when the inevitable occurs, you can't simply tighten them back down and expect to return to zero. You usually need a complete re-sight because if one loosens under recoil it takes the tension off the other and it often loosens also. If you have these mounts and your gun starts showing significant horizontal dispersion on the group, you can bet it's the windage screws. In fact, unless you're really fanatical on tension checks, count on it happening at some point.

Mount systems that use windage adjustment screws must be constantly checked for tightness. If one screw loosens, horizontal stringing will result.

Another drawback to this system is that to reach the base plate screws on this mount, you have to loosen both windage screws and remove the rings/scope from the rear base, and often the scope itself from the front rings. That also means a re-sight and you had better have a wide target, since there are usually no gradation marks on the windage screws to guide you to properly re-centering the scope. Your best bet is not to even start sighting in at 100 yards. Start at 25 to get the windage screws properly set first, then extend the range. During the thirty or so years I've been hanging around hunting camps and lodges, this type of scope mount has caused more problems than all the others combined, and takes the most time to correct.

Loose screws aren't uncommon on any scope mount system. Recoil will do it, and so will vibration. Slip a rifle into the gun rack of a jeep, ATV or swamp buggy, drive around for a few days, and don't be surprised by loose screws. You can help prevent that by making sure the bases and rings are properly mounted. Clean the screw holes and screws with a de-greaser (rubbing alcohol and cotton swabs work great), and then apply a thread-locking liquid to them. Don't use a permanent (red) type. Use the medium strength (blue). The red versions make it very difficult to remove the screws. The blue holds well, and allows the bond to be broken with hand tools. The more problems you can prevent at home, the fewer you'll encounter in the field.

STOCKING UP

If a review of the ammo and the sight mounts don't cure the problem, the next potential quick fix is to check the stock bedding screws. This is very important with a bolt-action rifle because the bedding screw tension affects the contact points between the action and barrel within the stock. Change that and barrel harmonics can change, which can produce poor groups and a shift in the impact point. In most cases, a rifle will shoot best with moderate, hand-tight pressure, but vibration can loosen those screws. Start by checking tightness, correcting where needed, and shoot a group. If the problem isn't cured or greatly diminished, you can try varying the tension on the action screws and a forearm screw (if one is present) . . . but my experience is that's usually a waste of time and ammo, unless you know through previous testing that certain degrees of screw tension produce the best accuracy in your rifle.

If your rifle is one that uses pillar bedding, screw tightness is critical. Maximum accuracy generally occurs when the front and rear action bedding screws are firmly tightened.

I once shipped a tack-driving, pillar-bedded rifle off to a smith to have a match trigger installed, and when I got it back I couldn't wait to get it to the shooting bench. I expected great things, but instead got group sizes that more than doubled. The ammo was the same match loads the gun loved, the scope mounts were tight, and I was left scratching my head. After all, the gun had just come back from a well-known gunsmith. When I finally got around to putting a screwdriver to the two action bedding screws, I discovered the front screw was very loose. I cranked it down and the rifle immediately returned to one-hole groups.

One additional stock problem isn't really a problem in the strictest sense of the term. On rifles with a two-piece stock (separate forearm and butt stock, as is found on many lever actions, single shots, and some semi-auto actions), if the front sling swivel stud is mounted on the stock forearm instead of a metal barrel band—and if the gun is sighted in with the forearm resting on a sand-bagged support, and then subsequently fired with a tight sling on the forearm wrapped around the shooter's support arm—the point of impact can shift.

I once owned a lovely little Ruger #1 single shot in .25-06 that would toss factory loads into tight little one-inch groups from a bench. If I dropped to a prone position with a tight sling it would still shoot one inch, but the group would be five or six inches low.

When a sling is used on a two-piece stock with the front swivel stud mounted on the forearm wood, it can alter the forearm pressure on the barrel, change barrel harmonics, and give you a point-of-impact-shift. Some two-piece stock designs are more susceptible to this than others, but all can be affected to some degree. It's something to keep in mind if you shoot this type of rifle. Don't automatically conclude you have a gun problem. It may just be the sling pressure.

One other potential "sling" problem is rare, but it has happened. Many rifles have a front sling swivel stud on the forearm. Some are just screwed into the stock. Others, however, go through the stock and connect to a nut in a recessed cutout within the barrel channel. If that stud extends upwards enough through the nut to contact the barrel, accuracy goes to hell in a hurry. I know of two instances where this occurred in a gun fresh from the factory that was incorrectly assembled. In other cases, it can occur through age and wear. Wood can compress over time, and if the front sling swivel stud gets loose, shooters tighten it. If the wood (or synthetic stock) compresses enough, and the shooter keeps tightening the sling stud, barrel contact can occur. If your accuracy suddenly takes a nose dive, this is something to check. If it has occurred, just file down the protruding end of the stud so that it doesn't contact the barrel.

TIME TO DIG DEEPER

The above quick fixes will handle the vast majority of wacky rifle problems and can take little time to diagnose and correct. If they don't fix the problem, however, it's likely one of those un-common but complex things that can really ruin your day. The least egregious possibility is that your scope has gone bad.

Scope reticles can start wandering around on their own. It's not common at normal shooting ranges with a quality scope, but can happen with less-expensive brands. For reasons I'll explain in a moment, it is quite common (even with a high-quality scope) when one tries to obtain a zero at extended ranges; i.e., 600 yards and beyond.

The reason is that traditional scope design uses opposing springs within the windage and elevation adjustment turrets to hold the settings you put in. Some newer designs incorporate firm mechanical locks, but many scopes still rely on just springs. When you crank in clicks of elevation (or windage) with these traditional spring systems, you are compressing the internal mechanism against one or more springs on one side, while addi-tional springs expand on the other side to maintain tension. If these springs weaken or break, the tension is lost and the reticle is free to "bounce" around under recoil.

Both windage and elevation seldom go at the same time. What often happens when your scope decides to travel this path is that you start getting either extreme horizontal or vertical dispersion with each shot. Recoil is moving the reticle and it's not likely to be in the same place twice. You can't fix that yourself. The scope needs to go back for repair.

At extreme ranges, the reticle can also "bounce" (in fact, it's properly called reticle bounce) but it's not due to a broken spring. Nor is the scope truly malfunctioning, although it appears to be. What is actually happening here is that the scope adjustments have been moved to their maximum position and the opposing spring tension is not strong enough to keep the reticle locked in place under recoil.

Every scope has a finite range of adjustment. This is normally expressed as "minutes of angle." One minute of angle is about one inch at 100 yards, or ten inches at 1,000 yards. The minute-of-angle adjustment range is generally stated in the scope literature. When a scope leaves the factory it is usually centered in the middle of that range. For the sake of a number, let's say a scope has a 60-minute adjustment range. When shipped from the factory, it will be set midway. That means thirty minutes of movement are equally available up, down, right and left. In theory, that means you can move the bullet impact point thirty inches at 100 yards or 300 inches at 1,000 yards. However, in the real world you seldom get that much.

As you approach maximum adjustment, you lose full spring tension on one side. I have a high-quality scope that cannot achieve a zero at 700 yards on my Model 70 with standard rings. The reticle bounces, and bullets wander all over the place. Drop it back to a 600-yard zero, though, and it stays dead on, with consistent 3.5-inch groups right on point of aim. There is nothing wrong with the scope other than my attempts to overextend the adjustments beyond their operating limits.

This is well known among experienced long-range shooters and military snipers, and the solution is simple: shim the rear rings to raise the rear of the scope. Now you are not zeroing at close range at a midway setting. You are using the lower thirty minutes, making them as well as the upper thirty minutes available to play with. Burris makes rings with shim inserts for just this purpose in their Signature Ring line. If you have sixty minutes of total adjustment range available, and you can achieve your close-range zero ten minutes up from the bottom, you now have fifty minutes of elevation to use—or 500 inches at 1,000 yards. That's a whole lot more than 300.

If you are trying to zero at long range and getting reticle bounce, but not at shorter ranges, your scope is fine. You just need to shim it to allow you to use the full range of adjustment.

If you are shooting at normal ranges and getting extreme vertical or horizontal dispersion, it may be a broken scope. Or, it may be something else. The quickest way to determine if it is the scope is to slap on another scope. If you are using the integral rings or the Weaver system, this is simple. If you have a spare scope already ringed up, attach it and shoot a group. If the group is as it's supposed to be (even if it is not precisely to point of aim) you've cured it. The scope was the problem.

With the other ring systems it's a bit more time-consuming to remove one scope and slip in another, but it's the only way you'll know whether or not the scope is the cause of your wacky rifle. If you are an experienced hunter you will likely have (or will want to have) a spare scope ringed up and sighted in, then removed until an emergency arises. It may not shoot precisely to point of aim when re-installed, but it will be close enough for you to quickly re-zero and get back in the game. An inexpensive fixed 4x scope and a set of rings is not a significant investment—and if it saves a hunt it's worth a lot more than it costs. Even if you are using the rings I don't like, a spare scope is still an excellent idea. It just takes a bit longer to install and zero. Regardless of which you use, it's a good idea to have a spare scope, because they are not indestructible.

NOW IT GETS BAD

If you've gotten this far without fixing the problem, it is likely to be something that is beyond your capabilities. There is obviously a significant problem in the barrel, action, or in the stock bedding (if you are shooting a bolt action). A trip to the gunsmith is recommended here, but before you go there are a couple more things you could try.

With a bolt gun, it is possible that problems exist within the bedding system, caused either by wear or the stock warping. This action type depends upon several areas of critical fit between the action and the stock. If that fit is incorrect the barrel harmonics are altered and accuracy suffers. The problem could be in the rear tang and recoil lug areas, the barrel channel, or a combination of both. It's not always straightforward, because how one portion of the action sits in the stock can affect other portions. Solving this is best left to a smith, but there is one area that might be fixed at home: the barrel channel on a free-floating barrel.

There are three primary methods for bedding the barrel in the barrel channel on a bolt gun. The first is fully bedded, in contact with the stock for the entire length of the channel; the second is bedded around the action and chamber, free-floated to within a few inches of the tip, and then contacted again; and the third is the chamber bedded with a fully-free floated barrel. If your rifle is bedded with the third option, it is possible that stock warping is putting a small section of the stock in contact with the barrel, and you can fix that.

To determine if you have a free floated barrel, put the rifle in a cleaning vise, take a dollar bill, and (starting at the tip) slide it back between the barrel and the stock to the chamber area. If it'll do that, you're free floated. If you feel a heavy resistance point along the way, that could be your unwanted pressure point.

Most action bedding problems require professional assistance. If, however, you have a free-floated barrel and warping has raised some contact points in the barrel channel, you can fix that yourself.

You can relieve these pressure points with sandpaper, regardless of whether your stock is wood or synthetic. To precisely identify them, remove the barreled action from the stock and apply a coat of Durrie Sales' Prussian Blue or inletting black (both available from Brownells) to the underside of the barrel. Then, very carefully lower the action back into the stock while keeping the barrel perfectly parallel with the stock until it is properly seated. Snug the action bedding screws down, let it sit for a second or so, then carefully remove the barreled action again.

Any high points in the barrel channel that are contacting the barrel will now be marked in the stock with the blue. Do not put any blue on the chamber area or any of the contact points just ahead of it; they are supposed to contact. You only want to find the unwanted high spots within the forward barrel channel itself. These can be sanded down to remove the pressure points. It will take several stock insertions with blue to show you with certainty that you are now fully free floated. If your stock is wood, be certain that you then seal the sanded areas with a quality stock finish/sealer. Wood stocks are normally the ones that will do the warping and mess up a free-floated barrel.

That's as far as I would recommend anyone go with kitchen-table bedding repairs. Anything further is best left to a professional.

If you haven't solved the problem by now, the chances are excellent that you won't, because barring recoil lug bedding problems that a gunsmith needs to correct, the culprit is likely the barrel. About the only thing you can do here is a full-blown, maximum-effort barrel clean as detailed in Chapter 2 and hope that solves the problem. Unfortunately, if you have been maintaining your barrel properly, it's not likely to have much effect. Even if you haven't been cleaning periodically, it may not save you either. I have a classic example sitting in my gun safe.

It's a sleek little 6mm Tikka Sporter that I ran across twenty-five years ago while working in a local gunshop. The owner couldn't get it to shoot, didn't like the caliber anyway, and wanted to trade. The bore was pristine, the action tight, and the trigger exquisite, so I acquired it. An inspection showed that the accuracy problems were likely the result of a "kitchen table" bedding job—perhaps done by the owner in an attempt to fix what he perceived as poor accuracy, or by the shooter from whom he obtained the gun. Regardless, it wasn't right, so I routed it out, glass-bedded the action, free floated the barrel, and added a touch of glass for forend pressure. The little Tikka turned into a one-incher and I hunted with it for a year or so before losing interest in the caliber. When a good friend of mine fell in love with it, he wound up with it.

My friend is a serious and highly skilled deer hunter, but he's not much of a gun nut. I doubt seriously if he fired more than a box of ammo a year during the twenty-three years he had the rifle; just enough to check the sights and take his season's limit. I also seriously doubt if he ever cleaned the barrel, although he assured me he did properly clean it on occasion. Knowing him as well as I do, I suspect his definition of "occasion" was once every four or five years, and his version of "proper cleaning" was nothing more than a powder solvent-soaked patch or two swabbed through the barrel.

That's not good, and it ultimately caught up with him last deer season. He went to the range to check the sights and found his groups in the six-inch range at 100 yards. He brought the rifle up to my range and we did the ammo check. Not the problem. I had a scope ringed up that would fit his bases, so we rigged it up and shot. No difference. I popped the action out of the stock and the glass bedding was no different than when I'd put it in a quarter century before.

I suspected what was coming next, and when I checked the bore it was like looking down a black sewer pipe. It looked like "The Bore From Hell."

After three days of maximum-effort cleaning, I could see enough of the lands and grooves to determine that the barrel was trashed. Deeply pitted from neglect, it was like looking through a coil of barbed wire. There is no fix for that. And I'm certain he didn't put more than 1,000 rounds through the gun the entire twenty-three years he owned it. He didn't shoot it out. It was just neglect that trashed it.

Even if your bore is in better shape than that, the barrel could still be the problem. Damage to the crown will do it. Excessive erosion just forward of the chamber is another death knell. If crown damage is all there is, a smith can cut and re-crown it. Beyond that, a new barrel is needed.

Re-barreling a rifle is less daunting than some think, but don't even consider the possibility of doing it yourself. Most barrel makers won't even sell you the barrel unless you are a licensed gunsmith. A barrel needs to be installed by a competent smith so that it can be properly chambered, headspaced, bedded, and test fired, and there are a number of companies that do it.

E.R. Shaw is one of the best known, and at their current prices a new stainless steel barrel installed, chambered and test fired on your rifle is around $300. Blued steel costs less. Compared to the price of a new rifle, that's not bad. And, if you like the rifle anyway, and the action and stock are in good shape, it's worth considering.

You also aren't locked into your present caliber. You can have it re-barreled to virtually any cartridge within that basic cartridge family. With the Tikka, its original caliber was 6mm, which is nothing more than a necked-down 7mm Mauser. So is the .257 Roberts. Either would require nothing more than the barrel be chambered for them, with no action or bolt work needed. If your caliber is based on the .308 family (.243 Win, .260 Rem, .308 Win, .358 Win) any of these can be had, and it's the same for other families.

That may be an extreme way to cure a "wacky" rifle, but if the barrel is trashed it's the only effective option other than a new rifle. Regardless of which option is chosen, at least you can now start the barrel out right.

FIXING IT IN THE FIELD

7

Many things can happen to your rifle on a hunt,
but with a little forethought you can fix all
but the most catastrophic breakdowns.

'm old enough to remember the once-popular TV show
"MacGyver", and I know I'm not alone there. It was an
interesting show. The basic premise was that our secret-
agent hero (MacGyver) would wander around the world with
nothing more than what he had in his pockets. He was prone to
get into all sorts of trouble that required complex equipment to
get out of, but he would then scrounge around to find the raw
materials he needed to make that equipment right there where
he was. A daunting task, but he always managed to pull it off,
and I wish I had taken notes. About all I remember now is that
ingenuity is good, and you can't go wrong with duct tape.

Maybe the reason I didn't take notes was that ten years of
military training had pretty much ingrained within me the con-
cept that "if you think you might need it, it's a good idea to bring
it with you." That's why I routinely carry a compact repair kit
that allows me to handle virtually any field emergency that isn't
so severe as to require a gunsmith.

Unfortunately, it doesn't take much in the way of a temporary lapse in judgment to bring on a "MacGyver moment," and one of my most memorable occurred some years back when I was invited out to South Dakota for one of those "gun writer" hunts.

Prairie dogs were the targets, and everything was to be provided. Guns, ammo, rests, earmuffs, binoculars, lunch, airfare, lodging, transportation, guides . . . you name it, and I didn't need to bring it. I was basically told to get off the plane with clothes, camera and a shaving kit, and that's what I did—leaving my field kit some 2,000 miles behind me.

The trip was going along quite smoothly until, at some point during the first afternoon, a sharp gust of prairie wind blew my "provided" rifle off its rest on the hood of my host's SUV and sent it spinning to the ground. Fortunately, there was no damage to the sights or stock, because when the rifle landed it went muzzle first into the soft black dirt and stood there quivering like a tossed javelin.

That's actually the best way it could have landed because the only problem now was about seven or eight inches of dirt rammed into the bore, and that's simple to fix. All you have to do is knock the main plug out with a cleaning rod and then run a couple of wet patches through to push out the dirt remaining in the grooves. It's about a 60-second job, at best. But when I asked my host where the cleaning gear was, I realized life wasn't going to be that simple today. Of all the equipment they'd remembered to bring, the one thing they forgot was the cleaning gear.

Since the nearest town where we might have purchased a cleaning rod was over an hour away, the rest of the afternoon was looking rather bleak. That's when MacGyver spoke to me from the other side of the broadcast aether.

I'd noticed that my guide had a shirt hanging up in the truck, so it got tossed onto a seat, and the wire coat hanger on which it had been resting became mine. Seeing as how he was the one that had forgotten the cleaning gear (and it wasn't his rifle) he didn't object. It took awhile to get the hanger more or less straightened out, but it eventually became a de facto cleaning rod and knocked the plug out. A look down the bore showed dirt still in the grooves, and you do not want to try and shoot that out. Under a best-case scenario it'll get it out; start to figure "worst case" aspects to that course of action, and bulged barrels, or worse, become a possibility. It wasn't my rifle, but I did need it functioning for the next two days of the hunt.

A wet patch would have been nice, but anyone who forgets a cleaning rod probably isn't going to remember patches, and that was certainly the case here. I thought about introducing my pocketknife to his spare shirt, but figured that might be pushing my amiable host a bit too far. So, after some rummaging around, I found some aluminum foil that had wrapped part of our lunch in the cooler. A piece of the foil plugged the muzzle, another formed a funnel, and a water bottle provided the liquid to pour down the barrel. Once that had set for a minute or two and moistened the dirt, I balled up enough foil to make a relatively tight-fitting "patch" and shoved that through the barrel with the coat hanger.

MacGyver would have been proud of me. It only took about thirty minutes, I found everything on site, and it worked. That was also the last time I went on any shoot without a basic repair kit. Playing MacGyver can get old in a hurry, and I darn sure wouldn't want to have to clean one of my personal rifles with water, aluminum foil, and a coat hanger.

A simple but effective field repair kit doesn't take up much room. It just requires some forethought, and one of the first things to consider should be a cleaning rod.

Just how sophisticated a cleaning rod/system you need to tote on a hunt depends on how often you expect to actually have to clean the bore. If you're up to your belt buckle in prairie dogs for a few days, or on a three-week African safari, you can expect that the bore will need proper cleaning every few days. You can also figure that under those circumstances your rifle is going to be traveling with you in a solid hard case that leaves plenty of room for the quality one-piece rod that you should have in your gun room. Why not bring it? And, while you're at it, carry the required brushes, jags, patches and solvents. If you have the room, it's nice to have serious cleaning gear with you.

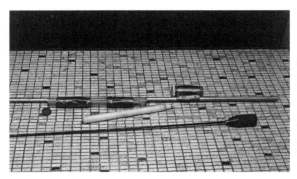

A full-sized cleaning rod will fit into your rifle's hard case. Note how the author has taped containers for the bore guide and brushes onto this Dewey cleaning rod holster.

It's true that not every hunt is going to dictate the need for that level of cleaning capability. No one seriously expects to have to clean their bore on a deer hunt that starts and ends in their driveway on the same day. Actually, even a multi-day hunt won't usually see a need to clean the rifle. But a bore obstruction is always a possibility. It's not hard to drop a rifle, or to trip and plant the muzzle in mud, snow, or plain old dirt (a strip of adhesive tape over the muzzle can help prevent that, and a small roll of tape also rides in my repair kit). Less common, yet still possible, is a defective load that can leave a bullet lodged in the bore.

Any bore obstruction stops the hunt, but a cleaning rod fixes things fast. This is one case where one of the little blister-packed, three-piece cleaning rods is worthwhile. They cost little and don't take up much room. Even more compact is the Atsko collapsible Rapid Rod I carry. This is a stainless steel rod with a steel cable running through it. When stored in its little pouch it's about the size of a large penknife. Pull it out, twist the knurled handle, and the cable tightens the individual sections into a 26-inch rod. It's tough enough to knock out a stuck bullet, and it accepts standard brushes and jags. There's also enough room in the pouch to jam in a jag and a dozen pre-cut patches.

A collapsible Rapid Rod, a few patches, and a small bottle of solvent/lube can fit in a shirt pocket and handle many barrel emergencies.

Along with that, I carry a little one-ounce plastic bottle of Speed X. It's the same basic formula as the other Corrosion X products and can be used as a light-duty bore cleaner, a lubricant for action parts, spread on a patch and wiped over external metal as a rust preservative, or used as a barrel preservative. All are useful, but the latter especially so. I have been in situations where bringing the gun into a warm cabin from frigid outside temperatures, or bringing it out of an air-conditioned lodge into a very hot and humid climate, would trigger massive condensation and almost immediately begin to promote rust in the bore. Patching it with the Rapid Rod and Speed X stopped that in its tracks. That not only prevented possible bore damage, but maintained accuracy.

The Rapid Rod and Speed X will fit into the same shirt pocket and—short of a full down-to-bare-metal bore cleaning—will do everything a full-size cleaning kit will.

Sights are another perennial field problem. Whether scope or iron, they can get knocked, dropped, stomped on by a pack horse, banged up by an ATV, or just decide to break on their own. Often, it's loose mount screws that are the culprit. Having experienced various iterations of these, I now include the screwdrivers and hex heads needed to handle each screw in the mount-and-ring system. That's not a big package, because a precisely fitting gunsmith screwdriver isn't required in an emergency. It doesn't have to fit exactly; it just has to work, and you can replace a buggered screw head later. It normally takes only one or two sizes to handle the vast majority of the slot screw heads you'll find on most mounts, and won't cost but a couple of bucks at the local auto parts store.

If you have TORX head screws, though, don't neglect the exact size. It is required, and even MacGyver might be lost without it. There is a practical limit to what you can expect a pocketknife to do.

If scope screws do loosen up, how far the point of impact will shift depends upon the type of mount system used. Once you tighten everything back down, you will need to re-sight, or at least check the sights. The fastest way to assure getting back to where you were is to fold up a previously fired sight-in target and tuck it away with you. All you have to do is put that up against a safe backstop and fire a group at the same range (or very close to it) at which you sighted the target in. If it impacts on the group already on the target you're good to go. If not, adjust the sights so it does. It's a whole lot faster (and far more precise) than trying to remember, "was I two inches high at 100 yards?" . . . and then trying to accurately measure two inches without a ruler. With a previously sighted target, when the two groups merge you're home free.

I go one step further—if I'm on a distant hunt I carry a spare scope in rings. I have witnessed numerous scopes getting

A previously fired sight-in target can get you back to your zero quickly if scope mount problems arise.

killed in the field. Some involved vehicles driving over them, pack horses stepping on them, rifles tumbling down a ravine (sometimes while in the frantic grip of the owner who was accompanying it on the ride down the hill), and once a car door crushing one. But my favorite dead scope story happened closer to home.

I was in the elevated rear compartment of a South Florida swamp buggy one night working a Q-beam light. It was legal— not only were we all sober, but we had state-issued gun and light predator control permits to deal with the coyotes and raccoons.

In the seats in front of me were the driver and the shooter next to him. This particular buggy held the guns in racks over the hood, and there were several guns in there, muzzles forward. Raccoons got the .22LR and coyotes got the .223 or .22 WMR.

My light found the bright green glow of raccoon eyes; the shooter grabbed a .22LR; lifted it from the rack . . . and it went off.

Unfortunately, it went off just as the muzzle was passing by the elevation adjustment turret of a very nice 4-12 x 40mm scope. That particular piece of hardware was upper level and very well made, but a point-blank hit from a .22LR exceeded its design parameters. The sparks were interesting, and that was the end of that scope. I'm glad I was in the back, and I'm also glad it wasn't one of mine.

Stuff happens. But a spare scope puts you a bit ahead of the curve when the really ugly stuff happens. Having even an inexpensive fixed-power model on hand can save an expensive hunt.

A spare scope already ringed up takes little room in a kit bag, and it can save a hunt.

I carry my spare scope wrapped in a small sheet of the bubble packing wrap you can get from any office supply store that handles UPS or Federal Express shipping, and then stuffed into a short length of PVC pipe that has an end cap glued to one end, and an end cap on the other secured with duct tape. It's compact, rough-handling-proof, and it'll float. There's also room in there for patches, screwdrivers, a folded sight-in target, and other small items. It takes a little room, but it's very useful to have along.

For the truly equipment-paranoid (which is not a bad state of mind to be in if you're wandering a long way from anywhere for an extended period of time), carrying a couple of spare base plate and scope ring screws, especially windage screws, isn't overkill. You can slip a lifetime supply into a 35mm plastic film canister, tuck it away, and never realize it's there until you need it. I have yet to see a scope system screw vibrate completely out and become lost, but I've heard of it happening.

Optics don't have to break to be rendered useless. All you have to do is coat a lens with mud, blood, campfire grease, oil, or just the fog that results from rapid changes in temperature and humidity. If you can't see clearly through your scope, binoculars or range finder, they may as well be broken. Even if you can see in most circumstances, a seemingly minor coating of crud (especially oil, even facial oil) can cause light flare under some sun angles. If your scope flares as you are settling the crosshairs on your trophy, you're pretty much toast.

There are a number of lens-cleaning solutions (available at any optical shop) that will clean even the most stubborn oils and leave a coating that will resist external fogging. I've used Pentax Clear View for years and I'm still working on the original two-ounce bottle. A lens cloth is nice, but a clean bore patch works quite well when it comes to applying the solution. Another excellent option is Birchwood Casey's Viz Wiz. This is a small, foil-wrapped package that contains a chemically treated lens cloth. It cleans and protects as well as the Pentax liquid, but is quite a bit more convenient. Tuck a couple of these away, and dirty lens problems are solved.

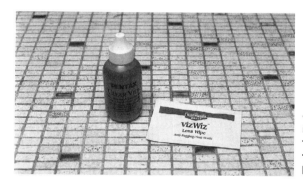

Lens-cleaning materials are often overlooked, but if you can't see through your optics, they may as well be broken.

Iron sights don't fog, but they can break, and carrying a spare (if it can be screwdriver-replaced) is smart. If your iron

Iron sights are sturdy, but can break. A spare is a good idea on an extended hunt.

sights use fiber-optic inserts, carrying replacement rods is doubly smart. These are more fragile than the sight itself, but on
many sight makes a broken light pipe can be replaced in seconds.

Most systems I have seen and used have a section of fiber-
optic rod (the light pipe) slipped into a fixture that holds it at the
front and rear, allowing the pipe to be exposed in the middle to
gather the light that makes it glow. Give that part a whack and you
can break the pipe. I have never broken one in the field, but I have
these sights on some of my competition handguns. I have managed
to break some of them at matches when shooting through a port
caused the recoil to bang the pipe against the top of the port.

Brownells offers extra light pipes, and replacing them is
easy. Use a penknife or small screwdriver to remove the broken
pipe. It's easy to push the pieces out either end of their mounts.
Don't try to cut the replacement rod to fit—just slip in an over-
length piece from the rear, extend it about ½₂ inch past the forward bracket, then lift the rod sharply. It'll break cleanly at the
rear bracket. Push the front edge back so you have an equal
amount of light pipe extending from the front and rear brackets,
and then heat each extending end with a lighter or match. That
will melt each end into a small blob and secure the new pipe in
place. It sounds low-tech, but that's exactly how gunsmiths do it
(at $50 per hour, or more, shop rates), and it's a solid installation.
A 35mm film canister holds the proper-length spare pipes well.

If your rifle uses a detachable magazine, a spare is handy.
They seldom break, but it's easy to lose them—if you do, you now
have a single shot.

It doesn't take a lot of gear to be able to handle common
field repairs. It just takes some thought, the knowledge that
things can—and do—happen, and the understanding that Mac-
Gyver was just a TV show.

It's always easier, and far quicker, if you bring your gear
with you.

LIST OF MANUFACTURERS

Atsko (Rapid Rod)
2664 Russell Street
Orangeburg SC 29115
(800) 845-2728
www.atsko.com

Birchwood Casey (maintenance & gun refinishing products)
7900 Fuller Rd.
Eden Prairie MN 55344
(800) 328-6156
www.birchwoodcasey.com

Break-Free (cleaners, lubricants & preservatives)
13386 International Parkway
Jacksonville FL 32218
(800) 433-2909
www.break-free.com

Brownells (cleaning, maintenance & gunsmithing supplies)
200 South Front St.
Montezuma IA 50171
(800) 741-0015
www.brownells.com

Corrosion Technologies (Corrosion X)
PO Box 551625
Dallas TX 75355-1625
(800) 638-7361
www.corrosionx.com

ER Shaw/Small Arms Mfg (barrel work)
5312 Thomas Run Road
Bridgeville PA 15017
(412) 221-3636
www.ershawbarrels.com

Gunslick (cleaning supplies)
N5549 County Trunk Z
Onalaska WI 54650
(800) 635-7656

Harris Engineering Inc. (Bipods)
999 Broadway
Barlow KY 42024
(270) 334-3633

Hughes Products Co. (bench rest bags)
4422 Wallburg Road
Winston-Salem NC 27107
(336) 769-3788
www.hughesproductsco.com

Iosso Products (bore paste)
1485 Lively Blvd.
Elk Grove IL 60007
(888) 747-4332

Kano Laboratories (Kroil oil)
1000 East Thompson Lane
Nashville TN 37211
(800) 311-3374
www.kanolabs.com

Michaels of Oregon (Hoppe's products)
9200 Cody
Overland Park KS 66214
(800) 423-3537
www.michaelsoforegon.com

NECO (pressure lapping)
536-C Stone Road
Benicia CA 94510
(800) 451-3550
www.neconos.com

Outers (cleaning supplies)
N5549 County Trunk Z
Onalaska WI 54650
(800) 635-7656
www.outers-guncare.com

Remington Arms Co. (gun care products)
870 Remington Drive
Madison NC 27025-0700
(800) 243-9700
www.remington.com

Sentry Solutions (dry lubricants)
33 South Commercial St.
Suite 401
Manchester NH 03101
(800) 546-8049
www.sentrysolutions.com

Shooter's Choice Gun Care (gun care products)
15050 Berkshire Industrial Parkway
Middlefield OH 44062
(800) 232-1991
www.shooters-choice.com

Tetra Gun Care (gun care products)
8 Vreeland Road
Florham Park NJ 07932-0955
(973) 443-0004
www.tetraguncare.com

INDEX

A

abrasive solvents, 10–13

accuracy

    ammunition, 85–88

    barrels, 97–101

    human element, 82–85

    scopes, 94–97

    sights, 88–92

    stocks, 92–94

Advance Auto Parts Carb &
    Choke Cleaner, 15

ammonia hydroxide, 11–12

ammunition, 60–64, 85–88

Atsko Rapid Rod, 106–7

B

barrels

    breaking in, 26–32

    cleaning, 32–33

    custom match, 26–27

    factory, 26–27

    function, 25–26

    lead bullets and, 38–41

    moly-coated bullets and, 33–38

    shooting accuracy, 97–101

bench tools

    drift punches, 20

    gun cradles, 20–23

    screwdrivers, 20

Birchwood Casey

    Barricade, 18

    Bore Scrubber, 13

    Gun Scrubber, 15

    Perma Blue, 70

    Tru-Oil Tung Oil, 74–75

    Viz Wiz, 111

    Walnut Stain, 77

Bix Stripper, 76

bolt actions, 46–48

bores

    guides, 3–4

    rust, 41–42

    solvents and brushes for, 14–16

Break-Free Carbon Cutter,
    15, 49

Brownells

    Acraglass, 71

    David Tubb's Final Finish
        System, 31

    Lewis Lead Remover, 7

    NECO Pressure Lapping
        Kit, 31

    Rust Preventative No. 2, 18

    screwdrivers, 20

brushes, 5–6, 8, 15–16

Butch's Bore Shine, 13, 42

C

carbon, 14–15, 49

carburetor spray, 15

cast lead bullets, 39

chamber brushes, 8

chemical solvents, 10–13
cleaning patches, 8–9
Corrosion X For Guns, 16, 17, 18,
        47, 52, 60
cotton swabs, 9
custom match barrels, 26–27

D
Danish Oil, 75
David Tubb's Final Finish
        System, 31
degreasers, 15
disassembly, 46
drift punches, 20
Durrie Sales' Prussian
        Blue, 98

E
equipment, cleaning
    bore guides, 3–4
    brushes, 5–6, 8, 15–16
    cotton swabs, 9
    jag tips, 6–7
    kits, 6
    muzzle guides, 4–5
    overview, 1–2
    patches, 8–9
    rods, 3
    slot tips, 6

F
factory barrels, 26–27
field maintenance
    bore cleaning, 104–6
    cleaning rods, 106–7
    repair kits and, 103–4
    scopes, 108–12
    sights, 108
    Speed X, 107

fire lapping, 31–32
Formby's Tung Oil Finish, 78

G
grease, 16, 18
gun cradles, 20–23
Gunslick
    Copper Klenz, 10
    Match-Grade Gun
        Maintenance Center, 21
    Ultra Klenz, 13

H
Harris
    Benchrest Model BR, 22
    Prone Model H bipod, 22–23
Hoppe's
    #9 solvent, 10, 15, 42
    Bench Rest, 10
    bronze-bristle brush, 8
    Elite Gun Cleaner, 13,
        15, 49
    Elite Gun Oil, 17
Hughes
    Ballistic Shooting Bag,
        23, 84
    Bench Buddy, 22
    Range Rest, 22

I
instruction manuals, 45–46, 47
Iosso Bore Cleaner Paste,
    13, 36

J
J. Dewey Manufacturing, 3
J-B Bore Cleaning Compound, 13,
        36, 40, 42
jag tips, 6–7

K

Kroil, 13, 41, 42

L

lead bullets
  cast, 39
  hard cast, 39
  new barrels and, 38
  swaged, 38–39
lever actions, 52–54
Lewis Lead Remover, 7–8, 43
Loctite Medium Strength Thread
Locker, 18–19
lubricants, 16–19, 59–60

M

manufacturers list, 113–15
Minwax
  Sanding Sealer, 78
  Wipe On Poly, 75, 77
moly-coated bullets, 33–38
Montana Xtreme Cowboy Blend,
    13, 40
muzzle crowns, 4–5
muzzle guides, 4–5

N

NECO Pressure Lapping Kit, 31

O

oils, 16–19
Outers
  Nitro Solvent, 10
  Scent Out Lube Oil
      Lubricant, 17

P

parts brush, 8
Pentax Clear View, 111

polyurethane finishes, 75
preservatives, 16–19
pressure lapping, 31–32
pump action rifles, 52

R

Remington
  40-X Bore Cleaner, 13, 36
  Rem Oil, 17
rimfires. *See* .22 Long Rifles
rods, cleaning, 3
rust, 18

S

safety, 15, 48
scopes, 94–97, 108–12
Scott's Liquid Gold, 73
screwdrivers, 20
semi-automatic actions, 48–51
Sentry Solutions
  Hi-Slip Grease, 18
  Tuf-Glide, 47, 52
Shooter's Choice
  All Weather High-Tech
      Grease, 18
  Copper Remover, 10–11, 42
  FP-10 Lubricant Elite, 16–17,
      18, 47, 52, 60
  Lead Remover, 13, 40
  MC#7, 13
  Polymer Safe Degreaser, 15
  Rust Prevent, 18
  Xtreme Clean, 13
shooting accuracy. *See* accuracy
Simple Green's All Purpose
    Cleaner, 72
single-shot actions, 54
sling swivel studs, 70
slot tips, 6

solvents
  abrasive, 13–14
  bore, 14–16
  chemical, 10–13
  multi-purpose, 13
  safety, 15
stocks
  cosmetics, 72–75
  minor repairs, 70–72
  refinishing, 76–79
  routine maintenance, 67–70
  shooting accuracy, 92–94
stress cracks, 71–72
swaged bullets, 38–39

T
temperature, 47
Tetra
  Gun Grease, 18
  Gun L, 18

thread lockers, 18–19
trigger assembly, 46–47
.22 Long Rifles
  action part lubrication, 59–60
  action part maintenance,
      56–56–57
  ammunition, 60–64
  barrel break-in, 55–56
  barrel cleaning, 56
  bolt face, 57–58
  bore preservatives, 64–65
  chamber, 58

V
varnishes, 75

W
WATCO Danish Oil, 75
water damage, 47
WD-40, 17

ABOUT THE AUTHOR

Chris Christian's shooting career spans over 40 years; beginning as a teeanager in Northern California where he developed a fascination with reducing the local ground squirrel and jackrabbit population with rimfire rifles and handguns—given that rimfire ammo was about all a 16-year-old kid could afford at the time.

The serious portion of his firearms education occurred during a 10-year stint as a Petty Officer with the U.S. Navy, where he spent a significant portion of his time as a member of Navy rifle and pistol teams and filled periods between matches by serving as a small-arms instructor. His education in firearms included attendance at both the U.S. Army and Marine Corps Sniper schools.

Following military service he settled in northeast Florida and began a career as a hunting and fishing guide, with occasional forays into predator control work. Christian is also an enthusiastic action pistol shooter, and currently competes in the Master Class with the International Defensive Pistol Association where he has won Regional Championships.

Christian has contributed over 1,000 articles on firearms and related subjects to magazines that include *SHOT Business*, *Outdoor Life*, *Field & Stream*, *Florida Sportsman*, *Guns & Ammo*, *Gun World*, and numerous others. This is the author's third book on firearms.

He currently resides on a multi-acre out-parcel in the middle of a Florida State Forest, where the firing range in his backyard gives him ample opportunity to do two things: shoot guns, and spend the required time cleaning them.